HEROES

AND

BUTTERFLIES;

Breaking Relationship

Patterns

By

Aimee Michele Semas, M.A.,

LMFT

Contents

*I*ntroduction

Why is it that we do the things we do, in relationships; act the way we do, make the choices that turn out to be poor to say the least? Although we usually don't recognize this until after the fact, retrospect is always 20/20. Yet we can look over at our friends, our comrades and muse over the decisions they make in relationships. To us on the outside it seems so clear. We know the direction they should and shouldn't go; yet they continue to make the same mistakes over and over again. Do you notice relationships that you have had with different people that take a similar course, that end up manifesting a specific outcome: one that tends to be the same outcome? A scenario of different faces yet the same story?

I have noticed patterns when I look around at the people closest to me as well as with myself. The question that continues to impede my mind is whether we can do something about it? I want to know how we can break out of these limiting roles, out of our relationship patterns. When we are in them they have a hypnotic pull, keeping us fixed in whatever pattern we are caught in, like a spider's prey. Once we are in the pattern our fate is pretty much set. Once the bait has lured us and our heart is involved we no longer have the freedom to just walk away unscathed: to do something different, to make a different choice. I am convinced that if we fall into the pattern we are to remain there until the dynamic unfolds through its natural sequence of events. Usually by that time we are worn out, emotionally drained and at a loss as to what happened. This is the time when we feel so far away from ourselves. The time when we realize that we lost ourselves and we must begin to pick up the pieces and rebuild the person we once were. At least that is what I have always done, until I began to realize how to avoid the pattern from happening and taking hold of my life. The key to avoiding, or rather releasing, your relationship patterns involves understanding where you came from, what impact your past experiences have had on your development and then healing past scars and traumas so you can begin to live a life of choice. Once this process has been successfully completed you can then consciously train yourself to do something different: this sequence is the key to breaking the pattern once and for all.

The essence of this book deals with healing and breaking our patterns in relationships. I will look at the nature of patterns, where they come from, and how to create new, positive and flexible ways of relating to others in your life. I will invite you to use exercises designed to provoke self-awareness that can guide you toward creating new ways of relating to others.

Through personal reflection and self-growth you can begin to choose the partners that will enhance who you are instead of preventing you from becoming your authentic self. The first step toward your spiritual freedom is discovering what patterns keep you imprisoned to relive your past. In order to begin that journey we will first explore the nature of patterns themselves; how they manifest and what purpose they actually serve in our lives.

*T*he nature of patterns

Why do we make the choices we do when it comes to romantic partners? Why do we create patterns in our interpersonal lives? Is it our fault that things turn out the way they do, one failed relationship after another? At first it is really tempting to absorb heart break and let it determine our self worth. After all we are the ones that either do the hurting or are hurt ourselves. When we are caught in a pattern and the relationship doesn't work out our instinct is to blame ourselves or aggressively blame the other because we don't really know why it didn't work out. Isn't it the other person's fault? Or is it because of some tragic flaw in our personalities that our relationships take a turn for the worse?

What if I were to tell you that it is our 'fault' or rather what if I were to tell you that actually it is the emotional climate inside of us that 'attracts' the drama out in the world. So in a round about way we do have responsibility for our failed encounters in the sense that it is because of unhealed wounds from our past that lead us to create the scenarios in our relationships that we do. In fact what I have come to believe is that we actually strive toward recreating our childhood encounters with those we meet when we are adults. I know this sounds Freudian and terribly cliché but it is actually a very real phenomenon that can be understood through using an analogy of how a bird launches into adulthood.

How a baby bird survives is through containment within its nest; this nest, built by its parental birds, serves as a place of safety and protection. It enables the baby bird to grow into adulthood. Its surroundings, its nest, represent survival and fundamental it is all the baby bird knows. Now let's imagine or pretend that the baby bird is pushed from its nest perhaps too soon, or injecting the human experience in this scenario, imagine its pushed from its nest before its developmentally 'ready' to leave the nest. If it were human, how the baby bird would respond to this event is by going out and trying to rebuild a nest that is a replica of its childhood nest. This of course makes sense because again it is the only environment it has ever been in, and this familiarity represents safety. The bird doesn't really understand any other way to build a nest, so it relies on what it knows; it builds the same structure it was raised in, in order to feel stable, experience a sense of comfort and ultimately complete its development so it can fly; so it can successfully launch from its nest. Now, we may ask why the bird would be motivated to create its original nest if the nest was essentially painful, or traumatic? This is where the analogy moves more to the human experience. So pretending as if the baby bird is a person the question of why it recreates its nest is twofold: first it is what the baby bird knows (it has developed an internal map in terms of how the world feels and how it experiences the world), and second (from a more object-relations psychological perspective) deep down in the birds unconscious it believes that if it can recreate the nest it had as a child it can then relive the experiences it had with its original nest differently. And if it can do it differently perhaps it can redo its painful childhood experiences; enabling the bird to develop successfully and finally move forward into adulthood.

Applying the nest analogy to our human experience, we can say that patterns in our relationships really reflect our attempts to create a replica of our childhood; and our attempt to finish our emotional/ psychological development. What happens in human development is that if we experience certain traumas before we are able to develop into emotionally/ psychologically healthy individuals our development is somewhat halted. We can't really move forward. We remain emotionally stuck at age 8, 12, or 14. Unhealed trauma keeps us developmentally arrested at whatever age the trauma occurred, so from this lens human beings recreate their original nest in order to set up the right conditions so they can complete their development and enter adulthood. This is where the idea of being pushed from the nest too soon enters, because for most of us when we turn 18 we are nowhere near ready to go out into the world and create healthy conscious relationships (and if we are developmentally arrested at a younger age, we aren't psychologically or emotionally really 18). So for human being we go out in the world in order to structure our own human nest so we can complete our emotional development, make different choices, and ultimately have more fulfilling relationships. Quite simply, our human nest becomes our pattern(s) in romantic relationships.

Perhaps the analogy of the baby bird is helpful or maybe you need to see more concrete examples. We will explore this idea further throughout this book but the main thing to keep in mind is that we make the choices we do in our intimate relationships in order to heal childhood wounds and become free, spiritually connected human beings. Because of this it is crucial to reflect on our past experiences, in order to gain insight into our childhood climate and in order to understand the dynamics we are destined to recreate in our adult encounters.

$W_{hy\ go\ back?}$

Let's face it everyone has had difficult life

experiences. This is the case with everyone I know,

for some their scars stem all the way back to their

relationships with their parents and/or siblings, for

others they were hurt by peer relationships or other

caretakers in their lives. Living in this world we easily

get hurt and disappointed and these experiences are

imprinted in our psyche. This is why it is so

fundamental to reflect back on our past in order to

understand exactly what *is* imprinted in our

unconscious. Now it's important to recognize that we

don't analyze our past in order to hold someone responsible for our screw-ups or our dysfunctional relationships rather we go back in order to recognize what is keeping us from moving forward; and to better understand the dynamics within our childhood nest. Once we understand what our nest was, we can begin to see how it matches with the conditions of our relationships today. Then we can begin to heal and eventually we will have to power to do it differently, to choose relationships that are free from the constraints of yesterday.

Inevitably we need to reflect on the past in order to process the traumas of yesterday, so we can open up more fully right now in the present moment. The thing that has always amazed me is that people don't want to talk about their childhood, referencing the notion of living in the moment, to live for today; while ironically

all the decisions they make are because of what

happened yesterday. We don't want to talk about our

childhood yet we are still behaving out in the world as

we did when were 5,12 or 17. Ultimately if we can just

begin to touch our grief, process it and understand it,

we won't need to act it out and then we could truly live

in the 'now'. So lets go beyond the proverbial

Freudian 'blame the parents or the world' stance and

reframe this phenomena in an amazingly uplifting

light: there is not reason to blame anyone because what

can be done now is actually a gift. If we remember our

past, pinpoint what our childhood dynamic was, we can

begin to see how we are recreating this in our adult

live. Once we do this then we are free to make more

satisfying decisions in our adult lives, and then we are

free to have fulfilling intimate relationships.

Anais Nin said, " We don't see the world as it is, we see it as we are." The whole process of sifting through the past may seem futile to begin with but ultimately it holds the potential to open us up to a new world; a world that can be as free as we are. Quite simply put if we limit ourselves the world will follow suit. Or as the Buddhist saying goes: "The world will treat you in the exact same way as you treat yourself."

Patterns in relationships, the ones that are painful and repetitious aren't really 'wrong', yes they hurt and are frustrating but they serve us in a huge way: for they inform us, or have the potential to inform us (if we become aware), of un-dealt with, unprocessed scars from our past. Once we have this information we can begin to heal those scars and choose a different course. You see when we are creating patterns in our relationships we are acting out the past in a way that render us choice-less, we get pulled to

certain partners and make certain decisions very

unconsciously. That is why we have to appreciate

how our intimate relationships can teach us about our

emotional climate; since our adult relationships are

likely a replica of our childhood dynamic they have

the potential to help us discover what childhood

interactions keep us stuck from making different

choices. Intimate relationships, especially ones that

hold a similar pattern, serve as a mirror of what's not

yet healed or what remains blocked inside of you. This

is a huge breakthrough because we have finally figured

out a way to discover material that has been otherwise

inaccessible to our conscious minds, through looking at

who we attract and are attracted to as well as how we

respond to those individuals. Let's explore more in

depth how past traumas, issues or scars can come to be

replicated in one's current relationships. In order to do this we must look more closely at the nature of human emotions themselves.

T he nature of emotions

It has been documented by numerous

researchers and theorists that repressed emotions have

the potential to create utter chaos in our lives. This is

because what is repressed will act out through our

interpersonal lives until they are processed. We may

ask how on earth my own emotional history can 'act

out' in my current relationships? Or, How can a

moment in my childhood where I was hurt or

conflicted come to affect what I do as an adult? These

questions can be answered with clarity once we

understand the nature of emotions themselves. In order to do this we will have to analyze the way emotions live and function within us.

The word e-motion linguistically depicts the nature and character of emotions: they are internal experiences or energy that move within our body (e-equaling energy and motion being movement: hence 'e'motion). We get feelings and internal sensations that are felt within us and ideally are expressed to the outer world. Our emotions come to the edge of our bodies and naturally seek outward expression. The flesh is at the edge of our inner world thus the body will display our inner experiences: it is moved to tears, trembles with fear, clenches in anger or smiles in joy. As mind/body theorist Catillejo put it: "Emotion always has its roots in the unconscious and manifests itself in the body" (Castillejo, quoted in Macnaughton, 1998, p. 114).

I look at the healthy or natural process of emotions as an active loop where the emotion is ignited internally and follows a course of movement through the body. This sequence is followed by an externalized expression and an acknowledgement of the emotion. Take for example the emotion of sadness. Sadness manifests internally, it then moves through the entire body (the lip may begin to quiver, the eyes soften, and the breath speeds up), these movements prepare for the action of crying to be expressed, where the person cries and then hopefully verbalizes and acknowledges what is wrong. Each emotional state follows a particular path of motion that will likely vary from person to person but the one universal process is: motion through the body leading to an outward expression that strives for external validation, understanding and acceptance. These last three steps: validation, understanding and acceptance of the emotion, is the moment when the individual gets insight into why he or she is experiencing the given emotion through telling another person and experiencing some sort of validation of the emotion which leads to an understanding and acceptance of that emotion. These final three pieces are a crucial aspect of the entire sequence. If these steps don't get completed then the emotion is not fully processed. This is important to note because the validation, understanding and hence acceptance of emotions are something that most people don't get the opportunity to truly experience during conflicting events in their life. So the loop looks something like this: feeling the feeling, expressing the feeling, sharing the feeling and finally understanding (validating) the feeling which leads to an acceptance and a simultaneous letting go of the feeling; which naturally happens if the emotional loop is truly completed. So if this emotional loop is left incomplete the emotion is kept from truly being released and processed. For example, if the person feels the emotion and even expresses the emotion outwardly (i.e., crying) but doesn't really process the emotion verbally, so there is not validation or insight into what caused the emotion (thereby understanding /acceptance/ surrendering), then the sequence is incomplete. So what happens when this sequence is incomplete? The answer is that the emotion stays inside of us; instead of moving outward and being released it is held inside. The way this occurs is through what has been termed as "repression".

In the early 1900's Sigmund Freud coined the term repression to explain how emotions are held inside of us instead of being expressed to the world.

This is the phenomena of holding emotional energy inside so it cannot express itself outwardly. When we do this we don't really realize we are repressing the emotion, for repression necessarily occurs when we don't achieve insight into why the emotional reaction is occurring. As Freud discovered when we repress we pretty much do it unconsciously (not only that but in order to successfully repress anything we *have* to do it unconsciously- if we didn't we wouldn't be repressing). It is also important to note that in most, if not all, instances we repress because it is necessary for our survival in a given situation. Take grief for example; it is impossible to fully express this emotion in its entirety when it is first felt because the emotional energy is so potent; if the person did express it, it would likely overwhelm them and leave them unable to function in the world. Also a lot of times we don't have the cognitive development to be able to complete the sequence. For example, if you are 5 years old and you experience the death of a parents you are likely too young to be able to articulate what your emotional reaction is; because of this you will necessarily have to repress your emotions in response to this event. So in a lot of ways when it first occurs, repression is absolutely adaptive. But even though it is adaptive when we initially do it we are still halting an emotional loop which leads us to be left with an unprocessed emotion. Once we are unable to complete an emotional loop then the given emotion automatically gets repressed and is filed away inside of us. What tends to happen from here is that since we no longer feel the emotion we assume that the emotion is no longer there. Unfortunately this is anything but the case.

Contrary to what we may think an emotion that is no longer felt, but was kept from being expressed, does not go away. Abiding by the 1st law in thermodynamics, energy is never lost its only transferred. Energy always has to go somewhere, it doesn't disappear, and since emotions are energy (remember: 'e'motion) if it can't be released it stays within us. And in fact not only does it remain within us but it will begin to grow in intensity the longer it is kept from being released. So if you don't express an emotion in its entirety then you necessarily repress that emotion inside of you and then the emotion stays inside of you until it can be allowed to complete its loop of expression. From there it takes a life of its own because then the incomplete emotional loop looks for opportunities to be expressed. And it seeks out dynamics that resonate with the experiences that originally created the repressed emotion(s) because the emotion years to be felt, expressed, validated, understood, accepted and released. It's as if our bodies hold an emotional magnet; seeking to attract situations that will manifest or trigger the unprocessed emotional material (we will explore this more in depth later).

For decades it has been acknowledged that emotional repression takes root in the body this is why massage, yoga and chiropractic work can sometimes bring up emotional material. As a yoga instructor and CMT I can't tell you how many times people have laid down in a finishing meditation pose quietly crying, or how during a deep tissue massage people have reported experiencing an upsurge of intense and deep rooted emotions. This is because repressed, unprocessed, emotions remain in the body. Again abiding by the 1st law in thermodynamics, emotions that are not processed and released remain within us, and the place they remain is within the body. Further, relatively recent research also has revealed that while the body holds onto repressed emotions the mind seems to be doing the same thing.

In the field of neuropsychology it has been discovered that once we experience a trauma we imprint the responses from that trauma in the form of solidified neural pathways. These neural pathways then become so ingrained that they become our mode of responding to any situation out in the world that is similar to the original trauma. In fact not only that but we may even interpret situations in ways that resonate with the conditions of our early traumas.

Our solidified neural pathways not only mold our perceptions and interpretations of situations but in some ways actually create the outcomes of our interactions because of our perceptions and interpretations. This neurological discovery is huge for explaining how emotional repression leads us to replicate our childhood traumas within our adult relationships without notice. Let's explore how the brain works with the body in keeping us destined to relive the experiences of our childhood nests; making it so we respond to similar events, and create similar events over and over again.

*N*eural *pathways & patterns*

There has been a tremendous amount of research in neuropsychology that has uncovered how patterns work within the human brain. What happens is that once an individual experiences a traumatic event the responses they emit at that moment become solidified in the brain and become a neural pathway. It makes sense why this is a mechanism for establishing future behaviors and reactions; after all it is how we survived that initial trauma, so that way of being (responding/experiencing) becomes imprinted as the mode of responding/perceiving/interpreting similar events forthcoming. These ways of being become a fundamental way to continue to survive out in the world. What then happens in the future is that the individual naturally uses these responses again, when he/she is confronted with a similar situation. What this means is that the individual responds to outward stimulus with a certain chain of behaviors, these behaviors become associated with the given stimulus and the next time the individual is confronted with a similar stimulus the neural pathway will register the similarity and the individual will automatically emit the same responses. This is quite simply the brain's way of ensuring survival. So if an individual originally had a traumatic experience related to his father's anger and he responded to this event initially by withdrawing, he will respond to that emotion similarly in the future. Likewise if the individual became anxious at this moment in time then anxiety will become their solidified response to anger. It is important to note that the original experience only needs to be subjectively traumatic, meaning that it might not seem like a 'big deal' to me or you but to this person it was significantly impacting. We can see how patterns work in light of this discovery, because all a pattern is, is a serious of responses to similar situations that manifest a similar dynamic and outcome. Solidified neural pathways help to create this unfolding. Further, what makes a relationship pattern a pattern is that our behaviors as well as the other person's behaviors are almost identical to past experiences with other people (echoing the energy, the dynamic, of our past). What is interesting is that even though the pattern is embedded within us, other people we interact with follow suit. This is because we are inherently attracted to people that resonate with our past and because the way we react to them naturally has an impact on how they respond- which can mold them into becoming the perfect partner for our pattern.

In fact when we first meet someone, on some level, our brain registers that they are a match for our pattern, or the perfect actor for our play. Indeed it has been theorized that the more someone matches up with our past 'people' or past situations the more attracted to them we become.

Solidified neural pathways explain how patterns actually happen at the neurological level. When a neural pathway becomes solidified it will dominate, it will become knee jerk, second nature and highly unconscious. It actually makes sense how repression naturally happens along with this process, for again when we repress we have to do it unconsciously. And a solidified neural pathway supports us acting out in a very unconscious way. This is a key discovery in neuropsychology which explains why our patterns and triggers become second nature and it all has to do with our autonomic nervous system: the part of the brain that is invested solely in our survival.

What has been discovered about human behavior is that we learn new behaviors quickly when a threat is present. The part of our brain that takes over during life threatening moments is known as the reptilian brain (a part of our autonomic nervous system) and its sole focus is to keep us alive. The responses that come from the reptilian brain are: fight, flight, or freeze. That is all it knows how to do. The part of the brain that is responsible for coming up with solutions, assessing how to respond to the environment in a way that takes into account consequences (the neocortex) is not accessible when the reptilian brain is activated. In fact they call it the reptilian brain because its responses are primitive and basic. All species have this defense embedded in their neurology; after all its sole purpose is survival.

When the autonomic nervous system is activated and the reptilian brain takes over, all other cognitive, as well as physiological processes, are dismantled. Now it makes sense that this part of the brain takes over during traumatic or life threatening moments; if a deer were to walk by a lion's den it better run like hell IMMEDIATELY. After all time is of the essence, so the dear being able to instinctually get away quickly seems fundamental to ensure escape. Other processes, like reason, problem solving and assessing consequences could actually get in the way of this primitive defense because it would take away the primary focus of survival. It's the same for human beings: as soon as we perceive something in our environment that is similar to a previous traumatic situation, our reptilian brain is activated and whatever ways we survived in the past will be utilized once again. The key difference between humans and animals is that traumatic moments don't always consist of physical threats or abuse, in fact for human beings as a species we are usually scarred the deepest from traumas that are emotional in nature.

The evolution of our species is marked by our ability to feel and verbalize our emotions and thoughts; the ability to self-reflect existentially and to have emotional reactions to situations. Perhaps some animals do have emotional reactions and they just can verbalize them, I couldn't really tell you but what truly differentiates us is that for human being we feel things

deeply, tell ourselves things about what has happened

to us and hold onto these things in memory and in

repression. Emotional trauma for human beings

interacts with the brain the same way physical danger

does for animals: it ignites our reptilian

fight/flight/freeze responses, and when activated this

rules our perceptions, interpretations and resulting

behaviors- and it does it QUICKLY. And because

access to the higher brain, the part of the brain that

thinks logically, is dismantled during this process the

behaviors/perceptions/interpretations that are ignited

happen without us even thinking about it. Again our

reptilian brain isn't wired to our higher brain that

enables linear logic and reason and because an

emotional threat feels like a threat to our survival our

autonomic nervous system kicks in without regard to

what our neocortex has to say about it. When our primitive brain is triggered we don't have a choice, we will respond the way we have learned unconsciously to respond because it has ultimately enabled us to survive the original trauma. And the responses that are emitted by our reptilian brain- that were solidified neural pathways from our original trauma ultimately become our patterns in relationships. Our patterns ironically represent our way of surviving on some level yet this survival mechanism also highlights how challenging it is to 'undo' a solidified neural pathway for the main reason that we have to dismantle the highly unconscious, knee jerk, activation of our fight/flight/freeze response.

Neuropsychologists explain that once a traumatic event occurs an individual will imprint the sequence of their behaviors in their brain and this imprint becomes their map for how to response to similar situations in the future. This phenomena really explains more clearly exactly how repression comes to affect our adult lives, once trauma happens it is not only solidified in our psyche but it is also structured in our mind. And it's like the two are bound together, and they will remain transfixed until we begin to heal the original trauma(s) that lead to the repression and solidified neural pathway to begin with. This is an exciting discovery not only because it explains how repression and patterns work but also because it brings an understanding of how we go about healing.

The way to undo neural pathways is twofold: first healing the original trauma so similar situations will no longer activate the reptilian brain (or bring up emotional repression- again closing the loop of expression) and second to begin to create new neural pathways. The hopeful piece that neuropsychology brings with it, is the discovery that the brain is pliable, as we begin to heal old traumas we are more able to create new neural pathways. However, before we begin to discuss restructuring our neural pathways we must first complete all of the incomplete emotional loops from our past; and in order to do this we must begin to explore what traumas keep activating the reptilian brain.

Since our patterns represent the ways in which we act out unconsciously and our repressed emotions are the reason why we act out unconsciously; then the more aware we become of our patterns the more conscious we becomes. Also, the reptilian brain is only activated when we come from a place of fear; so the more we confront what has happened to us, the more we process the emotions around our traumas (achieving acceptance and surrender) the less we will feel afraid. Fundamentally our solidified neural pathways cannot be undone without completing our unfinished emotional business.

The 'goal' in healing relationship patterns is to complete the incomplete loop of expression for any repressed emotion, in order to begin to live consciously fulfilling lives and in order to have conscious and fulfilling relationships. Once we free ourselves from emotional repression we are also free to create new ways of being, new neural pathways. Mind/body theorist Ron Kurtz (1990) notes, "by bringing these experiences into conscious we will be able to know them, to complete them and to move on" (p.28). To know them and complete them is analogous to processing the repressed emotions and allowing them to complete their loop of expression. It is through expressing the emotion outwardly and through gaining insight in to the emotion (understanding and accepting the initial trauma) thereby processing the emotion on both a mind and body level of experience that enables this to happen.

What's funny is that this all sounds incredibly simply and easy right? Now try to access your repressed emotions. I'll give you a minute, serious close your eyes and see if you can find them. It's pretty difficult to do isn't it? If something is repressed, it's next to impossible to know what it is, if it wasn't it wouldn't be repressed. This is where the potential for healing arises within the arena of interpersonal relationships because we can uncover repressed emotions through the way we relate to those closest to us and ultimately through analyzing our patterns in relationships. Luckily we have a way to discover what is repressed inside of us: and that is through looking at our intimate relationships.

What is amazing and divinely inspired is that as human beings we seem to be attracted to those individuals that stir up the most unconscious material, potentially creating awareness of repressed emotions which also brings with it the potential to heal old wounds. I believe the silver lining beneath rebuilding our childhood nests out in the world is the ability to clearly see our past, so we can revisit and re-experience our wounds in order to complete the halted emotions within us. Ultimately this process holds the potential to help us complete our emotional development and ultimately to heal our childhood wounds.

The human drive toward healing through interpersonal relationships is absolutely brilliant yet potentially tragic at the same time; it's brilliant because it holds tremendous potential for healing yet tragic because most of us do not realize that we have created the relationships we are in. We don't really know that we can learn so much about ourselves from our intimate encounters. This lack of knowing not only dooms us to repeat our pattern (the recreation of our childhood nest) over and over again but it also represents missed opportunities for growth and self-fulfillment. But that is what this book is about: we want to understand our intimate relationships in order to heal our wounds, process our incomplete emotions and make better, more fulfilling choices. Let's look more deeply at how our relationships reflect what our emotional blocks, repressed emotions, and solidified neural pathways are.

*P*atterns: *our human nest*

Children's play therapy is a fascinating process to be a part of. What happens is that the child will act out with the toys or dolls what the child is working through emotionally. If the child was a part of a horrible auto accident the child will come in and play this scene repeatedly: they will have one car hit another car and the other car hit the first car over and over again. While the child is doing this the therapist is there verbally acknowledging and validating what the child is doing; thereby bringing insight and acceptance, so the emotional loop can be completed.

This process can go on for months until the child is finished processing the experience and the emotions around the experience. What happens then is they simply move on. I believe what happens in adulthood mirrors this process; but instead of acting out our repressed emotions with toys we do it with our relationships. Let's look more closely at this.

A woman I worked with in my clinical practice had the experience of feeling a tremendous amount of shame in her family dynamic. Her father left when she was a young girl and he barely kept in touch with her. After this occurred, she never felt as though she was good enough because she unconsciously assumed that he distanced himself because she wasn't special or lovable. What then happened in adulthood is that she began to chase after men that didn't pay her the time of day, leading her to feel great depths of shame. Now we can see how the dynamic in her adulthood is strikingly similar to her childhood relationship with her father as she is attracted to a similar type of man- the kind that is emotionally unavailable. This unrequited attraction leads her to feel unworthy and unlovable which resonates with her childhood experiences of shame and feelings of inadequacy. Now from a psychological perspective we can see that what is happening is that because she repressed her feelings of shame and inadequacy as a child, she is unconsciously looking for an outlet through these relationships. Not only that but she also developed a solidified neural pathway around this experience, so whenever she attracts an emotionally unavailable man she immediately blames herself and feels as though it's because she isn't good enough (this is her reptilian brain response). Even though this entire scenario is a recreation of her childhood she is convinced that it actually is because she isn't lovable or adequate- which literally keeps her stuck in a perpetual self-loathing place over and over again.

What is interesting is that we are drawn to what triggers our autonomic nervous system; instead of running from it we actually seek out what has hurt us in the past. This is where we differ from other creatures. For the woman in the above example it isn't just that she has a solidified neural pathway or a tendency to respond from a place of shame when she meets an unavailable man, but she will actually continue to attract this dynamic over and over. On an unconscious level this again happens for two reasons: in order to find some mode of catharsis and in hopes of finally being able to express and understand the origin of her feelings of shame and self- doubt, so these emotions can then be processed and released. The potential exists each time she enters a relationship to truly express her feelings of inadequacy and shame to the point of release and healing, but the key is her discovering where these feelings originated.

A dynamic that evokes a sense of shame is going to be a necessary component in her adult relationships because it holds a vital characteristic that corresponds to her childhood nest. Like the baby bird she is seeking situations that resonate with the climate of her past. She will likely continue to attract these individuals in her life until she heals the original wound, processes the emotional material and creates new ways of responding (hence new neural pathways).

The human psyche is an amazing thing, in fact it is so powerful that it creates scenarios in the outside world in order to heal or relieve its internal incompleteness (i.e., repression). Just like a child in therapy, we are playing out the scenario until we have been able to fully process our past experiences. In this light then every individual with whom you develop an intimate relationship with will likely come to reflect what is repressed inside of you. Relationships are like a mirror, in that they reveal our blocked emotional loops. Thus examining our intimate relationships present an opportunity to become more conscious of what is limiting us from being spontaneous, open, and free.

Emotional repression naturally limits our freedom to live in the moment and to choose how we want to respond in our adult lives. When we have past wounds that aren't healed we live in the present with responses made and developed from our past. We aren't truly in the moment, and I believe the 'goal' in life is to live in the present. When we aren't authentically expressing ourselves and our emotions we are holding back a

part of ourselves from our experiences. This is why we

end up with predictable patterns in our relationships: we

will keep being confronted with the same types of

experiences until we really 'live' that experience, and

express our responses to what is happening in a

complete way (completing the emotional loop of

expression). This is also why patterns in relationships

lead to unrelenting frustration and a sense of defeat:

because they will always end the same way if we don't

do something different.

If you notice patterns in your romantic relationships

know that you are merely acting out your childhood

nest and your psyche is really presenting you with

opportunities to live the experience in a more authentic

fashion. This means really feeling the emotions and

exploring where they come from; grieving that moment

in time once and for all and then you will be free.

Let's look more closely at how patterns show up and how they show up specifically in romantic relationships.

*P*atterns in relationships

For whatever reason, how life has been created, the principles that underlie our experiences seem to dictate that how we learn the quickest, in the most complete way, is through our most intimate relationships. It seems that if it was as easy as intellectual understanding then we wouldn't need the arena of interpersonal relationships to grow or develop. After all if this was the case we could easily do it on our own and maybe God or the powers that be just 'felt' that this wouldn't really solidify our self-awareness and spiritual evolution. We need to feel it and live it through a whole mind-body experience, which moves us beyond cognitive understanding. In this light, we have to appreciate that relationships enable us to tap into what is blocked inside of us.

The moments when we get extremely angry, sad, or shameful in our relationships not only enable us to release the held down energy inside of us, but as we are beginning to see they also provide an opportunity for us to become *aware* of *what is* really inside us. They hold the potential for us to gain a tremendous amount of insight into what is keeping us from being who we really are as unique individuals.

Couples theorist Harville Hendrix (1985) alluded to the idea of patterns in relationships with his concept of the 'Imago'. Hendrix theorized that we seek out individuals who will bring up or trigger our repressed emotions in a romantic relationship. Our 'Imago' is an internal image or map of the characteristics that our romantic partner should hold; characteristics that correspond to our caregivers' personality traits. It is conceptualized that the more an individual holds the characteristics of our Imago the more attracted we will be to them. Hendrix believed that we will seek out partners that resonate with the personalities of our childhood nest, individuals with positive traits from our childhood as well as individuals that hold the negative traits from our childhood (caregivers, siblings, peers etc...). The negative traits are almost more of a lure because he believed as well that we choose the relationships we do in order to become conscious of our unhealed wounds; which ultimately opens the door to healing and breaking our unconscious patterns.

The Imago highlights how intelligently organized

the human psyche is by explaining how we unconsciously seek out relationships that are most conducive toward our healing. And this theory also supports the notion that the trick to healing is through becoming conscious of our unconscious wounds. Once we do this we can begin to see the inherent dynamics within our human nest. For our repressed emotions come from our childhood environment; they are what make up the dynamics of our human nest, so the more we remember our traumas the more we can uncover what is repressed. Not only that but the more we uncover our patterns the more clear we get on what our reptilian responses are; moving us closer to being able to undo these responses. So for those of us that have stark relationship patterns we can infer what our traumas and solidified neural pathways are by identifying what pattern we live by. Let's get a better look at the idea of the human nest and how we develop relationship patterns by exploring some real life stories.

Through observing people close to me as well as reflecting on my own life I have found many dynamics, many relational patterns (childhood nests), that vary between men and women. Yet I have also noticed a trend among the genders. In the interest of providing examples of how repressed emotions and our childhood nests manifest in our adult relationships I will describe the relationship patterns I have observed between men and women. These patterns I have termed: the hero/ heroine, butterfly/ player and the male/female vampire.

*T*he Hero

Joseph Campbell, in his writing on mythology as a depiction of the human embodied experience, spoke of several overarching patterns embedded in the human experience. In his book, 'The hero's journey', he spent quite a bit of time on the pattern of the hero as a way of being that is a historic pattern rooted within the human psyche. The way I am using the term here isn't so much as seeing this as a universal way of being within the human experience as much as looking as it is a script that seems to manifest according to its resonance with one's childhood experiences.

The hero pattern I have discovered is directly tied to an unconscious pull to try to save one's romantic partner. The hero is specifically a role that a man takes on when he has an unconscious drive to save the woman in his life (note: I will use the feminine gender because the examples I use are real life situations- but please substitute for different sexual orientations for applicability). This is the man who goes for the woman who seemingly needs his help. The man who always ends up with a partner who doesn't have a job, has gotten kicked out of their house, or who needs help escaping a dangerous lifestyle of drugs or alcohol. This is the type of man who in meeting a woman who is involved in an abusive relationship will be pulled to save her from her circumstances and all other pursuits in his life take the back burner. He becomes the hero and saving the woman becomes his unconscious trigger that ignites a desire to engage and protect. This is a good time to mention that on the surface repressed emotions might not seem negative or painful; after all the hero is strong and stable, and capable of helping the damsel in distress right?

The most common mistake that occurs in life is our misinterpretations of situations; when we focus on another person's issues instead of focusing on the entire dynamic within the relationship and inevitably fail to see our responsibility in the situation. Ask yourself: what is my payoff from this dynamic? How is this relationship serving me? The bottom line is that we are drawn to those who are at the same place in their development; what we should or could be asking ourselves as well as the man who plays the hero is:

what are you doing in a relationship with someone who is not as stable or available as you? The answer is that we actually are just as wounded as the other for if we weren't we would be seeking out another who is emotionally available. As the saying goes, 'water seeks its own level'. So with the hero, on the surface he is strong, healthy and steadfast but beneath the surface he has many repressed emotions seeking to be healed.

When we look deeper into the hero's psyche, exploring his youth and the scars from his past, what we will discover is that at some point in time he experienced a situation where there was a woman in his life who needed saving. Maybe his mother was left by his father, or maybe she was physically sick, had mental health issues or was just emotionally wounded. The emotions that are repressed for the 'hero' are likely a feeling of helplessness and a feeling

of being ineffective and his defensive strategy

becomes fighting back and taking charge.

Take for example a client I counseled whom I

will call Jay. Jay grew up in a divorced family where

his father left his mother for another woman. When this

happened his mother was devastated and emotionally

distraught, however soon after she got into a

relationship with a physically abusive man and this

man became Jay's stepfather. Jay was very young

when all this happened, so young that he was never

really able to express, understand, achieve validation

and acceptance for his emotional reaction to these

childhood events. He stood by while all of this was

happening and felt helpless and weak, over time these

feelings, because they were left unprocessed, became

repressed.

The older Jay got the more invested he became in feeling powerful; in fact when he was a teenager he grew to be 6 feet 4 inches tall and weighed 240 pounds. He became fixated on increasing his strength whenever he could. And once he became old enough to date he began to attract romantic partners that needed his help; which we can understand since this element resonates strongly with his childhood nest. In one situation he met a woman who was in an unhealthy and dangerous relationship with another man (which really mirrors his childhood situation), in another the woman had a child and couldn't really take care of herself or her child's needs, the next was an exotic dancer and in Jay's eyes she wasn't safe and needed help out of this profession. In each scenario the underlying theme was the same: a woman needing Jay's help. This was the universal pattern that was present even when the overt circumstances seemed as though the woman didn't need saving. These situations are extremely revealing of how driven the psyche is to heal itself: Jay was seeking out a woman that matched the characteristics of his mother/father/stepfather dynamic, thereby seeking to rebuild his childhood nest.

What's interesting is that Jay did step outside of his pattern a few times: in one scenario he met a very independent and seemingly self-sufficient woman and what happened? He decided to move her to a new town where she knew nobody. As you might predict once this occurred she became very dependent and all the sudden 'needy'. She also became highly emotional and needed Jay's attention and validation constantly. How amazing is this? From this we can really see how people not only seek out partners that will fit the part in their unconscious script but they also create it; on some level they figure out how to change the circumstances in the other person's life in order to have the dynamic resonate more completely with their childhood nest. Another interesting piece is that once Jay wins the woman over and helps her and she becomes completely dependent on him he leaves the relationship. I'm guessing there are a few reasons why this happens. First, a woman that is reachable is someone who is stepping outside of the dynamics of his childhood. Meaning that since he was never able to help or reach his mother, a woman who is reachable simply doesn't match the dynamics. Secondly, an available woman would also challenge Jay's ability to connect intimately; which would be highly difficult until he dismantles his trauma responses. And finally when Jay leaves the relationship it's like he is launching himself from his childhood nest; perhaps trying to leave the dynamics of his childhood once and for all.

With Jay's situation the feeling of helplessness, which he likely feels when he is pursuing a woman that needs saving, is the main quality of his nest. This is the embedded neural pathway in his mind; a woman in need of saving triggers an unconscious feeling of helplessness which leads him to overcompensate by trying to save them- thereby decreasing his feelings of helplessness. These are the repressed emotions that are going to need to be addressed, validated, understood, accepted and thereby processed before he can ever successfully launch from his childhood nest. But before we go on to talk about how Jay can heal his repressed emotions and his unconscious pattern let's look at another example of the hero.

A friend of mine who I will refer to as Alex is

another great example of the hero. With Alex, he tends
to attract younger woman whom he tries to save and
take care of. At first the match seems perfect to him, he
feels a great sense of peace and excitement when they
meet. Then he begins to share with his friends tiny
little issues that he dismisses as unimportant: issues like
she is leaving for school two states away in three
months, or that she is taking a break from her boyfriend
but she still sees him here and there. Alex acts as
though he doesn't care about the outcome of the
relationship because after all he really just wants to
enjoy the moment, so he's kept from really reflecting
on the relationship's longevity and health from the
beginning. The pattern then becomes more intense as
he becomes deeply attached to the woman and strives to
integrate her more thoroughly into his life.

One situation Alex was drawn to was with an

extremely independent and recently made single girl, who just moved to the area a week before their meeting. She expressed to him immediately that she was not looking for a long-term relationship as she had just ended a tumultuous relationship back home. She also told him up front that she was unsure of how long she would be staying in the area. Alex played it cool when hearing this news; he told her that he wasn't looking for anything other than someone to hang out with. As he kept saying this to her as well as to his friends he began to confide in me that deep down he hoped that maybe he could win her over. In his mind he believed that if she began to love him then she would change her mind. Alex soon began doing things for her: fixing her car, helping her find a job and an apartment. He completely focused all his attention on this woman and his friends started seeing less and less of him. After a few months their relationship began to struggle, inherently because Alex's attachment to this woman didn't acknowledge her emotional unavailability. A month later this woman decided to break off their relationship because she expressed to Alex that she felt he wanted more from her than she could give. She expressed her process and highlighted that at this point in her life she needed to experience and explore her freedom. My friend reacts to this situation with self-blame and his self-esteem plummets while he is now emotionally devastated and heart broken. He can't understand what he did wrong; he thinks to himself that if only he was more supportive or loving she would have fallen for him. After all he is the hero, he is suppose to be able to save her; thereby winning her over.

As an outsider looking at this situation it is really easy to point out how obvious the outcome was.

After all she was clear with him from the beginning so why was he so devastated by her behavior? What was the payoff for Alex to stay in this type of situation when it was only going to cause him pain? How could he just ignore all the warning signs? This is where it gets interesting and where the pattern comes to the surface: if we explore with Alex his past experiences we will find what is motivating his choices or rather what is making it so he seemingly has no choice whatsoever.

After talking with Alex about this situation and all the other relationships he has had in his life we engaged in a conversation about his childhood. What I discovered was that this pattern is rooted in an experience he had when he was twelve. At this age his mother left his father; as Alex describes it 'she took off to chase after money and fame'. And up until this point in his life his mother has always been emotionally elusive, unavailable, and he still has difficulty maintaining a healthy relationship with her. Now we can appreciate why Alex attracts the type of women that his does when we look at his context. His mother was emotionally unavailable; he wasn't able to reach her as a child, so this dynamic is a fundamental part of his childhood nest. What is occurring in Alex's adult life is he is trying to rewrite his past and complete his emotional development by doing it differently in his adulthood (i.e., keeping the woman from leaving). But what he always ends up feeling is helpless and inadequate, which are his repressed emotions and I would say responding to these situations in this way (reacting to a woman who is unavailable with caretaking behavior) is a solidified neural pathway and a reptilian brain response for Alex as well.

Now we may ask how this is serving Alex at his point in his life, clearly it isn't because of the pain and devastation that is brought on by these relationships. But if we again look at his childhood context we can see that when he was a boy and he experienced the separation from his mother he was too young and he didn't have the appropriate environment that could allow him to express and process his emotions in a healthy way. So the relationships he gets into now in adulthood serve him because in them he is able to, on some level, express some of his childhood emotions of loss and abandonment. This is where patterns become more complex, because it isn't just that we learn how to be in relationships, meaning that Alex likely learned to be the hero in response to how his mother was. He also needs these relationships in order to perhaps begin to heal this painful experiences he had in his family of origin.

Now one would think that after a few heartbreaks, which are so painful and devastating, which lead us to express and experience difficult emotions on a daily basis that we have successfully expressed all of our repressed emotions. I mean grieving for months, everyday and every minute, would definitely be an authentic expression of our grief and loss from our childhood. But the thing is that once we have an emotive block, once we cut off an emotion's movement of expression, it grows in intensity. Meaning at some point Alex was probably told to be 'a big boy' and get over his mother's absence, at this point Alex had to cut off his grieving in order to adapt to his environment. Likewise Jay experienced a family dynamic where nobody could really discuss the divorce, nor could they acknowledge the abuse with his stepfather, so he also had to stifle his emotional reactions to these traumatic events. Neither individual had an environment that provided the safety, guidance and support to enable them to complete their emotional loops of expression. Therefore both repressed their grief, feelings of loss and helpless in order to adapt to their environment and as the years marched on the unexpressed emotions within them began to grow in intensity. Again if an emotion is not completely expressed, it remains stuck until it is expressed through the body and it is integrated into one's perspective or mind (insight, understanding and acceptance). So Alex then would not only need to express his grief but he would need to understand that the grief he is expressing isn't so much about his current relationship as much as it is about his experiences as a twelve year old boy. Likewise, Jay would also need to come to a place where he realizes that his drive to save the woman is something that is embedded in his unresolved conflict over what happened with his mother, father, and stepfather in childhood.

The reason why a pattern will emerge with people over and over again is because we grieve a current relationship in the present and move on; very rarely do we pinpoint what childhood event evoked the difficult relationship to begin with. Like with Alex, when I pointed out that the girl had told him in the beginning that she wasn't looking for a relationship (as this is what he told me when they first met) it was literally like he was hearing this information for the first time. Until one integrates the memories of their past and they understand the initial impetus to their relationship patterns, they are destined to live them out and they will live them out *unconsciously*. We can cry, scream, and sink down into a pit of despair only to eventually recover and move on but we will continue to act out our repressed emotions in our interpersonal life until we reflect upon our patterns. Not only that, but our behaviors will remain the same until we release the stored emotions that created the patterns to begin with. It's like a record that will continue to skip because there is a scratch on its surface, our emotions will continue to repeat themselves until we finally take the record off of the turn table and repair the crevasse by hand. But, before we start to explore ways to transcend the pattern, our reptilian responses, and create new neural pathways let's look at more examples of relationship patterns. And this time let's look at classic female response to the men out in the world: the heroine.

*T*he Heroine

The female counterpart to the hero is the woman who falls for the guy with a 'bad boy' persona. These are the women who give their time, their energy and their love to the men who seem lost and unreachable. This is the woman who struggles to wake this type of man up: to get him to realize how her love can change his ways. This type of woman I refer to as the Heroine.

One woman I know, who I will call Lisa, had this role down to a science. In one situation she found herself completely enthralled with a man whom nobody really cared for. He was the type of guy who was very attractive and intelligent but who was extremely withdrawn and angry. The first time she saw him she was at a party and he was the one standing in the corner: looking at all the people with an air of disgust. She found herself drawn to him and tried to make eye contact with him most of the night. Her attempt failed and she immediately felt an unshakeable sense of disappointment. She began to ask herself what was wrong with her to make this guy not notice her. What transpired was months and months of these types of interactions which led her to obsess about ways to get close to this man and each time she failed she began to feel more and more inadequate. Finally this man began to show some interest in her and she was elated. She soon found herself spending every minute of her day either thinking about him or doing things for him: she would clean his house, make his meals or do his laundry. She was his confidante, he would tell her all the things in his past that hurt him, and she was determined to help him heal his wounds. During these times she of course felt self-less; she felt as though she was the strong one and he needed her help. She became the classic heroine who was trying to save this man from his self-imposed prison.

Eventually the relationship ended when Lisa realized how this man was not the right 'match' for her. He began to become possessive and in the end the relationship turned ugly when he began to stalk her. She ended up getting a restraining order and left the relationship feeling as though she was lucky to be alive. Because of the way this relationship ended, because

Lisa really felt that it was his dysfunction that was the demise of their connection, she never really understood what unconscious pattern motivated her to bring this man into her life to begin with. We had a chance to discuss the situation which led us to naturally start a conversation about her childhood.

It turns out that Lisa's parents divorced when she was five. When this happened Lisa's father moved away and became physically and emotionally unavailable to her. Lisa always felt a strong connection to her father and she was devastated by his absence. On some level Lisa told herself that it was her fault that her father was no longer close to her so as an adult she began to unconsciously create scenarios with other men to match this painful dynamic. The overarching theme to her pattern was to fall for the man who was emotionally unavailable. Like the beginning of the last relationship I described, the dynamic where she feels unseen and inadequate mirrors the dynamic she had with her father as a child; and her response to this dynamic (winning the man over) also reveals the solidified neural pathway she developed in response to her childhood nest.

The next piece to her pattern is when she finally gets the man's attention and spends all her time and energy trying to please him (doing his laundry, cooking for him, being his therapist etc…). During these times she looses herself in the relationship because she is focused on keeping the man in her life close to her. Here she is acting out the heroine role overtly by helping the man with his emotional issues and personal chores but deep down she is doing it, not to help him, but to ensure that he needs her enough to stay with her. How a lot of her relationships end are also similar:

where she finally 'wakes up' and realizes how badly the man in her life treats her. She then leaves the relationship with a new found sense of self-esteem and concludes that it was because of her partner's flaws that the relationship ended the way it did. This aspect of her dynamic really reflects her unconscious wish to have had more control over the separation of her father from her family. When she is able to walk away she no longer feels like the helpless little girl who was left by her father; like Jay she is trying to experience the launching from her childhood nest.

It is also important to note that Lisa tends to get out once the relationship dynamic is no longer about her saving or trying to win the man over, like in the above example her partner no longer was elusive but became very possessive. And since this way of being in no way matches the dynamic she had with her father, it makes sense why she is no longer pulled to stay. It is interesting how a pattern has many nuances, going from one extreme to another, but just like our real life stories: each person's pattern unfolds many different emotional experiences. For Lisa the way her pattern manifests directly speaks to the unconscious wounds that have been buried inside her; her loss, her sense of rejection and her feelings of helplessness. When the relationship no longer holds these elements she 'wakes up' and moves on.

Ultimately the path toward healing relationship patterns begins with the retelling of one's childhood story. Once we do this we can begin to see the parallel between what happened to us as children and what we do now in our romantic relationships. Now let's look at another example of the heroine that will reveal the subtle and different nuances that manifest from similar life experiences.

Another woman, who I will call Emily, has a similar story to Lisa. She also is drawn to men who are unreachable. She too looked for the one man who wouldn't give her attention and she would pine after him. This was such a re-occurring pattern for her and each time the pining period would go on for months and months. But once she 'won' the guys affections she would suddenly withdraw. During these times she describes it as though she is completely unreachable even to herself; where she suddenly becomes very self-conscious and awkward in all interactions with her partner. This is a great example of how nothing in our relationships are clear cut or static; we may be one way at one time and then an opposite way at another. Emily's past explains more deeply where this paradoxical response toward her romantic partners comes from.

Emily also came from a divorced family where her father left at an early age. She had contact with him the subsequent years but she never felt the connection she once had with him when she was a young girl. She described to me that as she grew older and entered puberty she became very awkward around her father as if she didn't know how to be. Deep down inside I believe she was afraid to really be herself for fear of further rejection from her father. We can see how she unconsciously projects this dynamic into her adult relationships (and how this is definitely a solidified neural pathway, where withdrawing is her solidified response). She chases after the man, just like she wanted to do with her father as a child, but once she gets the man to develop interest in her she is afraid he will leave if he sees the real her. She had one relationship that was an on again off again dynamic

that went on for years. Each time she would pine for

the rekindling of the relationship, but once they came

together for a few weeks she would suddenly withdraw

and become distant. This response naturally led to the

demise of the relationship. What is interesting with

Emily is that this relationship remained back and forth

for years until suddenly her partner became the pursuer

and was the one that instigated the rekindling of their

relationship. What then happened was that when they

came back together Emily suddenly remained 'herself'

and her partner became completely available and

attentive. After a month or so she describes just

loosing interest in the relationship, like she all the

sudden fell out of love with him. From a childhood

nest lens we can see that what happened is that her

partner was suddenly available and attentive, which in

no way resonates with her childhood dynamic. Thus Emily, like Lisa, 'wakes up' and realizes that she is sadly not in love anymore.

As a child, Emily was never able to express her feelings of inadequacy and shame around her father leaving to anyone in her family, and these feelings are so complex that as a child they were difficult for her to understand let alone express. Thus she will continue to use her adult relationships as a venue to work through her repressed emotions and heal her childhood wounds, but this will only be possible if she becomes aware of how she is creating the dynamic to begin with.

It is interesting how different people experience similar events in such unique ways. We tell ourselves different things when events happen out of our control and what we tell ourselves impacts how we are going to be out in the world and how we are going to relate to others in intimate settings. Let's look at yet a few more

examples of common patterns between men and

women, this time let's examine the counterpart to the

hero and heroine, what we will call the player and the

butterfly.

T*he Player*

On the other end of the spectrum from the hero role we have the player. These are the individuals who seem to have an extreme disdain for intimacy and a fear of commitment. The player is the individual who runs from love with such ferocity and vigor; they go out, have a good time and try to get into some kind of trouble before the night is over. These are the men who dodge commitment at all costs yet they aren't conscious of their avoidance. It seems as though they feel they are only worthy when they remain aloof and untouchable. One man, I will call Jared, took on this role and he played the part of the player perfectly. He would go out and remain on the outskirts. He never really got too close to anybody. He would manipulate others in order to better his situation. He would date numerous women at a time all the while none of them knew about each other. Jared felt as though it was him against the world and he never really trusted anyone in his life.

How Jared's relationships would unfold is that some woman (likely a heroine) would come into his life with the intention of winning him over. She would be there for him in any way he requested. He would keep her at arm's length by dating other woman and keeping dates with her sporadically. Then what would transpire

is that eventually Jared would fall for one of his women

and then his aloofness would suddenly mutate into

possessiveness. What I learned in interacting with

Jared is that he came from a very tumultuous home

where his parents fought constantly, sometimes

escalating in physical violence. What happened when

Jared was a teen was that his mother died in a car

accident after she and Jared got into a fight. After this

event Jared unconsciously told himself that he was

responsible for his mother's death and on some level he

removed himself from the rest of the world. The

aloofness he displays in the beginning of his

relationships really echo this unconscious strategy

while the strong attachment he develops once the

woman gets close really speaks to his un-dealt with grief and ultimately his profound fear of abandonment.

When Jared becomes possessive over the woman in his life he is really acting out his unconscious wish to hold on to his mother thereby keeping his mother alive. It's as if he is so afraid of connecting to another person that at first distance is his way of coping with this fear (being the player) but once he finally gets close he has to hold on to her with all his might in order to keep himself from experiencing any sense of grief/abandonment. Jared is a unique case where his grief was so untapped and so repressed that he unconsciously was driven to not experience any type of loss. Likely because the feeling of loss in his present relationships would cause an avalanche of repressed grief over his mother.

A lot of times the player is the one who has been so hurt they have resolved unconsciously to just give up; on some level they are so afraid of intimacy that dating many women and remaining aloof is the way they deal with their repressed emotions and fear of abandonment. We will talk more about what the healing process might look like with Jared but first let's look at another example of the player.

Another example of the player is visible a previous client I worked with who I will call Eric. Like Jared, Eric was also involved with the darker side of life. He was always up for a party and would engage frequently in drugs and alcohol. He had too many tattoos to count and he prided himself on being an outsider in society. Eric rarely got involved in a long term relationship and when he did, like Jared, he would first remain completely detached and aloof and then when he got more deeply involved he would treat the woman in his life as if she was a possession, his possession. Once this happened Eric's indifference would mutate into abusiveness. He would also begin to spy on the woman and has confessed to reading his partner's journals or diaries. Eric didn't really understand his behavior during these times; after all he always identified himself as being cool and emotionally distant. But once the woman in his life won his heart he found himself completely obsessed with her whereabouts, as if she might all the sudden meet someone or disappear.

In talking more in depth with Eric about his behaviors in his relationships we began to explore his past experiences in greater detail. Turns out that Eric's biological father died at a very young age. He was actually so young he couldn't remember. Eric's mother eventually found another partner and remarried when Eric was around 8 years old. Eric was very attached to his stepfather and throughout his early teen years he describes himself as being very loving and motivated to be 'a good person'. The fatal loss occurred for Eric when his stepfather, like his biological father, died of cancer when Eric was 15. He recalls this event with a great deal of pain and anger and stated that after this event he resolved to never get too close to anyone. He, like Jared, felt it was him against the world and he consciously strove to keep anyone in his life at arm's length. Because of this resolve Eric could not understand why he behaves the way he does when he finally gets into an intimate relationship.

Looking at Jared's situation from a lens of the human nest we can understand first why he remains aloof and distant; after all these behaviors keep him safe from opening up to another person, defending against the possibility of feeling loss or grief. And we can also understand why he finally comes to feel his strong feelings of attachment and fear around losing the relationship because these are the true feelings that have been repressed. Eric was never able to process his grief attached to loosing his biological father nor was he able to express his loss and grief around loosing his stepfather. For Eric, his feelings of grief were so magnified, having lost both men in his life, the only way he could survive these feelings was to turn them into anger. When Eric would begin to treat the woman in his life abusively what he was inherently doing was defending against his great feelings of grief, sadness and fear of abandonment. It's as if he directs his anger toward the one person who may hurt him. Also he likely has a lot of rage around the fact that both his father and stepfather left him by dying, on some level he is probably expecting his mate to do the same.

I later learned that when both of the men in Eric's life died he immediately began getting into fights and becoming extremely aggressive with anyone in his path, I believe the reason he becomes aggressive with his partner is because this emotion represents a solidified neural pathway. However what is interesting is that because of his anger; because he is trying to defend against being hurt once again, what ends up happening is that he fulfills his fears of abandonment and the woman leaves because of his abuse. This is where his unconscious is trying to bring up the overwhelming amount of grief he has repressed inside for, like Jared, the person leaving is a fundamental part of his childhood nest.

Eric and Jared both have similar processes happening in the outside world; their defense is to keep people away in an attempt to keep them safe from loosing another person in their life. However, unconsciously they are motivated to really process the unexpressed grief that lies inside. This eventually leads

them into relationships that are destined to end. In an

interesting way this outcome makes it so they

experience the pain of loosing a relationship: they do

experience grief and sadness, however what they really

need to experience is their original feelings of grief and

loss around their parents' deaths. Once they realize

that the pain they feel in their adult lives is really

echoing their childhood losses they can then become

conscious of what is repressed inside of them. Once

this happens they can begin to process these emotions

on both the mind and body level.

It is interesting how different individuals can

experience similar tragedies in life and how he/she

responds to those tragedies with similar defensive

strategies. Both Jared and Eric acted out their childhood wounds in ways that mirror one another; yet there are also subtle nuances that make each one of them unique as individuals. With another individual who I will call Johnny, we will see that he personified the typical player on the outside, but deep down he was also a hero. Let's look at how this manifested itself and what happened in his childhood to create this pattern in his adult life.

When I first met Johnny he completely embodied all of the characteristics and behaviors of a typical player. He dated numerous women at once, would bounce from girl to girl even in one night and if he were out at a dance club or bar he's the guy that literally leaves the night with at least 5 phone numbers.

What was interesting about Johnny was that he always seemed to be drawn to a similar type of woman; she was usually older, by at least 5 years, and always was divorced or had kids. This seemed odd to me since Johnny was one of those guys that all the women loved, but he always seemed to hook up with woman who possessed these characteristics and life circumstances. I didn't think much of this pattern, that is until I had the opportunity to hear his story.

Turns out that Johnny was sexually abused by his female babysitter when he was 7 years old, and his babysitter was about 7 years older than him at the time. He recalled this story to me in a kind of matter of fact way; yet at the same time his affect relayed a sense of embarrassment hidden beneath a veneer of logic. When

I heard this piece of his story it hit me that there was a direct parallel between the older babysitter and the older women he had sexual relationships with. Further I also found out that Johnny tends to sleep with these women only a few times, and it's usually the women that dictate the when, the where and the how many times of their encounters. From the lens of the childhood nest it makes sense why Johnny relinquishes control around sexual intimacy. Due to the experiences he had with his babysitter this way of being in his sex life is a piece of his childhood nest (this response also being a solidified neural pathway). Further, I'm sure those moments in time when he was a child were very traumatizing for a young boy. Here he was in the safety of his own home, only to be sexually molested.

He likely experienced a lack of control around his sexual experiences with his babysitter and I'm sure he has a wealth of feelings repressed due to the violation of his personal boundaries.

The more I talked with Johnny the more I also discovered that in his adult life most, if not all, of the women he has sexual encounters with actively pursued him and many are extremely assertive if not down right aggressive. It makes sense why he is drawn to and attracts older, more aggressive women; women who are overtly assertive and ignore his personal boundaries. It's like his psyche is replicating similar circumstances of his childhood in order to bring his repressed emotions to the surface.

In talking to Johnny about the parallel between

his childhood experiences and his current encounters he

had a difficult time making the connection, which

makes sense because his feelings around the trauma

have been successfully repressed and outside of his

conscious awareness. What is interesting is that as he

talked more about his experiences in his adult

relationships he began to muse over the stark contrast

between his current lifestyle compared to how he has

been in the past. He shared that he actually has fallen in

love several times in his life and they are always with

women who, unlike his sexual partners discussed

above, are the ones that actually need a lot of re-

assurance.   He shared that these women lack the

confidence and assertiveness of the older women he

seems to play the role of the player with. I began to ask

him more about this pattern and this is when I found out that Johnny actually has astrong pull toward playing the hero as well as the player. Johnny disclosed that all of his past serious relationships were with women that needed his help: one woman was just getting out of an abusive relationship and another woman was dealing with the death of her mother. In both situations Johnny found himself bending over backwards to help the woman no matter what.

I started to ask Johnny more about his childhood. He relayed that his parents were divorced, although this didn't happen until he was older. This piece actually didn't make sense, until he began to share more in depth information about his parents' relationship when he was growing up. Turns out that his father used to drink quite a bit and was verbally and

physically abusive toward his mother. His mother was

very submissive and would take his father's abuse.

Johnny is extremely close to his mother and he even

relayed that he would stick up for her when his father

would verbally attack her. Now this information made

a lot of sense when applying this to Johnny's dynamics

with romantic partners, because he is naturally drawn to

women that need to be saved, thus behaviors that take

the form of protection are his solidified neural pathway.

Further it is interesting that the woman he settles down

with tends to be the one that needs help; with her he

plays the hero. Whereas the ones he engages in sexual

encounters with is the woman who is the aggressor and

with them he becomes the player (this really makes

sense since this resonates with the dynamic of his very first sexual encounter).

Of course when Johnny gets into serious relationships he is unconsciously fulfilling his wish to save his mom, and predictably what happened in all three relationships was that once the women he was with became stable he would end up loosing interest and the relationship would end. Again if we aren't aware of our pattern we will continue to act it out, so if you meet someone and they all the sudden switch roles on you (turning from submissive to assertive for example), you will either have to heal your old pattern or you will likely move on. Johnny didn't see the connection between the switching of the roles as playing a part in him loosing interest, he naturally blamed the end of the relationship on the fact that 'things just didn't work out'. This is our way of making sense of the course of events our relationships take, but unfortunately when we think this way we end up remaining the victims of circumstance. When we see our pattern as the main influencer of our relationships we suddenly gain a tremendous amount of power over what happens to us and our relationships.

Johnny is a good depiction of the reality that with human beings there are many complexities. With him he is drawn to certain women sexually (due to his sexual interactions with his babysitter), while he is drawn to other women when it comes to having a committed relationship (ones that resonate more with his feelings around his mom and dad's relationship).

Thus with Johnny he plays both roles; sometimes he is the player and other times he is a hero. Ultimately, both roles will continue to be his script until he begins to heal the wounds that created the patterns in his life to begin with.

When we reflect on these common patterns in relationships we have to appreciate that while some seem to be gender specific, in this day and age it seems as though men and women are free to take on the other gender's roles. Men have the social approval to become more emotionally sensitive and nurturing while women are free to become more logical and perhaps emotionally detached or independent. We are living in a time where there is a tremendous amount of freedom to live life the way we want and although many ways of being are ingrained in us as a gender we really do have the opportunity to take on different roles at different times. With this said let's now look at the female counterpart to the player role. These are the women who have taken on the traditional role of the masculine noncommittal who flutter from relationship to relationship in order to avoid commitment and intimacy. These women I refer to as the butterfly.

*T*he Butterfly

One woman, I will call Alyssa, personifies the role of the butterfly with such clarity. Her attitude toward intimate relationships is extremely nonchalant: she can take them or leave them. Her real drive in life, she would say, is her career and her dedication to bettering herself as a human being. After a long conversation with Alyssa I discovered that her scenario is this: she goes out and meets different men; they approach her, pursue her, and give her their phone number. She has a great time interacting with these men when they first meet but it never really goes further than that. She rarely calls them or lets it go further than a first date. A few times she did start to date someone, although she told herself not to get attached. In fact when she does start to really care about a guy she breaks it off; making up something about him that she didn't like, usually telling herself that she couldn't trust him. Alyssa has gotten to a point where she doesn't think she could ever be in a romantic relationship and she has resolved to just focus on her career. However, deep down Alyssa wants a family, she wants children and wants to settle down but she can't really bring herself to commit to any one person. When we look at Alyssa's past we can see what is fueling her lifestyle: speaking to why she pushes intimacy away with such energy and resolve.

When Alyssa was a child her parents were divorced, her father was unfaithful to her mother and he left the area to be with the other woman. Alyssa would only see her father a few times a year after this occurred. She told me that this wasn't really what has kept her from believing in love though, she shared that it was actually when she was 17 and her boyfriend died in a car accident. She told me the story and it also turns out that about 6 months after Alyssa's boyfriend died she learned that he was unfaithful to her right before he died. When Alyssa found this out a part of her died and at this moment she resolved to never trust another man again. This internal resolve was something that she never really thought about until our conversation, but when she reflected back she also told herself that she could never trust herself in a romantic relationship again either. Alyssa has suffered from episodes of depression and often finds herself experiencing a sense of extreme detachment; where she zones out to such a degree that moments are lost in time. Looking at her past experiences we can see how her defenses have really taken over her life especially in regards to romantic relationships. She keeps a safe distance from everyone around her and her moments of 'zoning out' I believe reflect a defense that enables her to distance herself from herself additionally. Further, the phenomena of withdrawal and extreme detachment are also a key emotional response that has likely become a solidified neural pathway for Alyssa as well.

Alyssa's depression speaks to her internal process, for if you stop to think about it, depression is an indication of repression: where you hold everything down to the point that it zaps all of your energy. However, depression is her secondary response to these events for her emotional detachment to others and to herself speaks to how she has dealt with her feelings of loss, grief and betrayal. Another interesting aspect of Alyssa's experience is what we discovered about her lifestyle as a younger woman, before her resolve to remain distant from the world kicked in.

Alyssa's story is complex because she became a butterfly as an older woman but when she was in her 20's she really took on the heroine pattern. She disclosed this information deeper into our conversation, and acted as though it was an unimportant part of her development. I found this fascinating because it really speaks to the repressed emotions inside her more directly. When she was in her late teens and early 20's Alyssa actually found herself drawn to men that were emotionally unavailable and involved with other women: the classic player. She confided in me that it amazed her how she ended up falling for men that are in other relationships, she said that it actually happened so many times, that she felt as though she was a magnet for the unfaithful. This phenomenon occurred even when she would clearly ask the man if he was involved with anyone and he promised her he was single; in these instances it always turned out that the man was less than honest. As she disclosed this information she still couldn't quite figure out what that pattern was about when she was younger. She also stated that these experiences were just another reason for her to not trust anyone, which led her to take more of a butterfly stance years later. Now looking into her past we can really see what motivated the pattern of attracting 'taken' men into her life. Because of her dad's and her boyfriend's unfaithfulness, Alyssa developed an internal desire to take the man away from the other woman.

Unconsciously, this is what she wanted to have happen

with both her father and her boyfriend. It's as if her

psyche felt that if this could be achieved she would

avoid experiencing her feelings of loss and grief.

So her acting this out in the world is really mirroring her

internal wish of redoing the tragedies of her past.

This is an amazing example of how our

unconscious will be drawn to individuals that match the

characteristics of our nest; Alyssa never knew these

men were involved with other women when she met

them, but on some level, some part of her did. There

was a part of her that knew these men held the dynamic

that matched her childhood experiences. Alyssa has

never processed her emotional response to either her

boyfriend's or her father's infidelity, she was too young

to know how to deal with her father's actions and so

overwhelmed by grief to begin to process her

boyfriend's unfaithfulness. We could even say that for Alyssa, attracting these types of men maybe even led her to feel the intensity of her feelings of betrayal so much that she eventually just gave up and decided to live the life of a butterfly: someone who doesn't get close to anyone. The pay off for this pattern is that she is assured that she will never get hurt; for the possibility of romantic intimacy is nonexistent if you don't get too close to anyone; and if you don't get too close you won't be affected if they cheat, die or leave. However, we can really see how her strategy to remain detached from any relationship is really a secondary response to her underlying wish to win the man back from the other woman.

Alyssa disclosed that all of her relationships ended when she successfully won the man over, shortly after this occurred, for her, the relationship dynamic would fizzle. It could again be reasoned that the relationship began to fizzle because it no longer held the unconscious pull of 'winning the man from the other woman' pattern; if Alyssa is with an emotionally available man not only is her pattern somewhat broken but then she is also placed in a position of emotional vulnerability. This is something that her psyche simply hasn't been ready for.

As we have discussed with the other patterns, in order for Alyssa to heal from her past wounds she could use these relationships as learning opportunities: because they reveal her un-dealt with feelings of loss, betrayal and grief. Ultimately once she begins to process some of these emotions she won't need to unconsciously act them out in her romantic life.

Alyssa and Johnny's stories are good examples of how the patterns we act out sometimes morph into another defensive strategy; we might first act out the

heroine/hero role only to be led to take on the

butterfly/player lifestyle. However, I have found that

the characteristics of these patterns are pretty universal.

What is interesting is it seems as though the player/

butterfly lifestyle may reveal more of a defensive

strategy rather than an unconscious pattern; meaning

that the player and butterfly themselves are defended

against getting too close to anyone and thus feeling any

emotion, repressed or otherwise. These individuals

have likely been hurt by their initial pattern so they

resolve to not engage in the game any longer; it's like

they remove themselves from anything that may trigger

childhood scars thereby remaining safe from feeling

anything. Healing for these individuals necessitates

looking deep into their past and discovering what their

initial wounds are, followed by exploring their

lifestyles when they were younger (i.e., their teenage years, 20's or even 30's) to see if they had a specific pattern originally, before they took on the detached stance of the player/butterfly.

Johnny's situation is pretty unique because his player tendency really spoke to the position he was put in as a young boy being forced into a sexual encounter with an older woman. For him being a player really corresponds to the dynamic of his first sexual encounter: having been molested by an older woman in a situation where the interaction was purely sexual likely imprinted in his psyche (and creating a neural pathway in his mind) of what sexual encounters should look like in the future. In his situation it is also interesting that all of his random sexual encounters never become serious relationships, it's like he keeps those two worlds separate; as this is what he learned.

Both Alyssa and Johnny's stories hit upon a phenomenon I have discovered with patterns; a lot of times one pattern can give way to another. Just like with Johnny and Alyssa there are those who morph from the butterfly/player into a more sinister type of pattern, which we will explore now.

There are two more patterns that have emerged for me as I have studied relationship patterns, and they seem to remain hidden until the individuals involved are deeply attached to their partner. This is the 'fatal attraction' pattern where the individuals involved become emotionally unstable, desperate and do things that are outside the norm of society. I call these individuals the emotional vampires: male and female.

*M*ale *Emotional Vampire*

The emotional vampires are the individuals who lack any trust in a relationship. They are the ones who feel as though they must manipulate the other in order to remain in control and in order to have their partner committed to them. They have a tremendous amount of anxiety with intimacy and in many ways I believe can be the shadow side to either the hero/heroine or player/butterfly pattern. With most that embody this pattern they likely have deep childhood scars that resulted from early traumas. Let's look at how this shows up in world by first examining the male version of the emotional vampire.

One individual I will call Chris on the surface embodied the player role to a tee. He was cavalier about all romantic relationships, kept everyone at arm's length and was as cool as he was nonchalant. In fact you would assume that Chris was one of the most confidant human beings around. However what I soon discovered after knowing Chris for some time was that he actually had another side to him that was the antithesis of cavalier. Chris would be completely detached and uninvolved with all women he would date, until one of them captured his heart. What happened then is that Chris would slowly start to control her life. He would limit her freedom by making dates with her frequently, he would call her 10 times a day as a way to monopolize her time and after a while he would check up on her by driving by her work and home. As the relationship evolved Chris would even start to snoop around her bedroom, looking into her purse and scanning her phone when she left the room. The relationship started to involve physical violence as well, as Chris would become physically abusive if she seemed unwilling to do what he wanted. Eventually the relationship became so intense that his partner broke up with him which led Chris to experience such anxiety that he stalked her daily. What resulted was a restraining order. However this did not stop Chris, he escalated even more leading him to attempt to kidnap her from her home. These behaviors went on for some time, in fact to this day if Chris even sees this woman he gets a strong emotional reaction (this of course indicates the dynamic still triggers a reptilian brain response in him). However to everyone else he meets

he has resumed the detached player stance once again.
Now looking at this scenario we have to wonder what
happened in his childhood to provoke such strong
attachment along with aggressive and life-threatening
behavior.

When Chris was a little boy his mother and
father would get into such extreme physical altercations
that his mother would be bruised and bloody. What
happened for Chris as he got older is that he would try
to stop the violence between his parents and numerous
times he was thrown aside, kicked, punched or slapped.
Chris soon learned to escape what was happening by
going to the arcades or the movies by himself.
Eventually he got to a point where he convinced
himself he didn't and shouldn't care. What happened
later in Chris's family is that his mom left his dad.
Chris was older at this time so he chose to live with his

dad and his relationship with his mom grew distant. Chris experienced a mixture of different feelings as a child; the feelings of helplessness mixed with aggression, abandonment and his secondary response of indifference. So in later years this shows up in his adult life as the player/vampire.

When Chris is single he displays the characteristics of the player perfectly; he is detached, unaffected and completely even keeled. However once he gets into a relationship he experiences so much anxiety around intimacy; this anxiety gives way to physical aggression and desperate attempts to prevent any form of abandonment.

When Chris becomes possessive of his partner, he is really acting out his desire to keep his mom from leaving, thereby undoing the pain of loosing his mother. The controlling aspect of his behaviors and the violence echoes the physical altercations of his childhood dynamic as well. When Chris was a child he responded to his father' abusiveness with aggression himself (by trying to stop his dad from hitting his mom); thus this behavior is likely a solidified reptilian brain response. Further what is interesting about Chris' pattern is that he only becomes controlling and possessive when the woman in his life is more detached. When the woman is available Chris plays more the player role: where he is indifferent. Once she starts to pull away Chris's anxiety increases and his pull toward the vampire is activated. This of course makes sense because a woman who is more indifferent and detached herself brings up the abandonment he felt when his mom left, which ultimately matches his nest.

Chris's pattern is a good example of how you never know all sides of a person, and quite frankly we can't judge one way or another. We have to appreciate that Chris, like all of us with relationship patterns, is unconsciously recreating his childhood in an attempt to heal his wounds. Jared and Eric also emulated this pattern once they get attached in their relationships as well. I would guess that the pattern of the vampire might be for those who have experienced more intense trauma. For example the death of a parent (or with Eric two parents) and for Chris the physical violence and his mother's abandonment likely created more intense ways of coping that lead each of them to act out in ways that are more aggressive and harmful. Also it seems that acts of physical aggression might *tend* to be a male response to feeling out of control and threatened. With that in mind let's now explore the feminine version of this pattern, the woman who displays aggressive and unstable behaviors more in subtle ways of emotional manipulation: the female emotional vampire.

*F*emale Emotional Vampire

The female version of the emotional vampire is the woman who manipulates the man in her life in every way imaginable. She takes a controlling stance similar to the male vampire but she does so in more emotionally or even sexually dramatic ways. She may seduce her partner, lavish him with attention and affection in an attempt to pull him in. One woman who exemplifies this pattern, who I will call Tina had this down to a science. She would lure a man in with her confidence and sensuality; lavishing him with compliments and building his esteem. She then began

to dominate his life completely; in one situation she

moved into his home within a month and took over his

whole world. Soon he was paying her bills and

spending every minute of the day with her. She would

keep her man satisfied by fulfilling any sexual wish or

fantasy; which almost kept her partner in a place of

hypnosis. We learn more about why Tina took on

these behaviors when we look into her past.

Turns out that when Tina was very young she

was molested by her father. What happened in

subsequent years is that her mother found out about the

abuse and left. After this Tina and her sisters lived

with her mother and saw her father rarely. What

happened to Tina was never discussed in the family

and because of the level of trauma Tina repressed this

event for years. It wasn't until her late 20's that she

confronted what happened. Tina then began to do exotic dancing to make a living and was highly promiscuous. It's interesting when we look at her childhood and compare it to her pattern later in life because we can see what repressed emotions she is unconsciously acting out.

Like all patterns, deep down Tina is conflicted over the events of her childhood. There is a part of her that seeks to have control over her partner due to the feelings of helpless she experienced around the molest; so the fact that she uses her sexuality to exert her sense of power makes a lot of sense. This element is common for a lot of women involved in exotic dancing or stripping, I believe it's a way for women to regain a sense of control over their bodies; and I have found that a lot of dancers hold a pattern of sexual abuse in their history. With Tina it is also interesting how her relationships end. In her last situation her partner

became completely passive; in this scenario she

disclosed that she lost interest in sex, and

even felt disdain for the man. This led to her break off

the relationship and leave. I believe this happened

because a passive man in no way resonates with her

childhood dynamic. Once she wins the man over

completely the lure to stay is no longer there. I think

feelings of disdain are also an aspect of her nest;

perhaps indicating the conflicting feelings she has

repressed around her experiences with her father. It is

also interesting that once intimacy begins to be

established her sexual attraction disappears; as if she

shuts this off perhaps to feel safe. I would guess she

has a lot of repressed feelings around what happened

and these feelings are naturally in conflict with one

another. What we can infer for certain is that her need

for control over her sexuality coupled with a fear of intimacy is at the base of her adult reptilian responses. What is also interesting with Tina is that her relationships with women also reveal a conflicting pattern as well.

In Tina's world she tends to respond in a black and white way toward the women in her life: she either loves them or hates them. This way of being really echoes her repressed feelings toward her mother: where she feels grateful for her protection but also resentful toward her for tearing her away from her father. As children we naturally love both our parents regardless of what they do or say. So if one of them hurts us in a physical or emotional way it is difficult to know how to feel. I believe Tina is struggling with this conflict internally. Thus both her relationships to men and women oscillate between extreme attachment and complete disdain.

For both Chris and Tina, the key to healing their relationship patterns is for them to explore their past traumas and begin to express their repressed emotions; thereby dismantling their reptilian brain responses. Because of the intensity around their childhood experiences, their healing will likely be a long and challenging journey. Highly traumatic experiences usually require a lot of containment and support, so with these types of experiences I would recommend seeking out a therapist or coach as a guide. What is important to remember is that healing is possible for anyone who is willing to go the distance. With the right tools and support we can all break the patterns that bind us; leading us to heal our painful childhood scars.

The patterns that unfold with all of these 'types' seem to occur in conjunction with their gender counterparts (whether a hetero/homo/bisexual relationship); meaning that usually the hero's 'fatal' pattern is to chase after the butterfly/female vampire, and the heroine's unconscious pattern is to fall for the player/male vampire. They exist and are viable only as long as their counterpart continues to play their complimentary role; meaning that only one person in the dyad needs to change, to do something outside of their role, to break the predictable dynamic between them. However once this happens the relationship will likely end if the unconscious emotions that were drawn to the relationship to begin with go unprocessed; yep the attraction will likely die and they will leave searching for the perfect counterpart to their pattern.

I have found in my own life that I have tried on different roles, I have been the heroine and the butterfly and now I muse over the likely outcome of each dynamic. The ending always being the same: where I am alone and the other is out of sight. In the scenario where I was the heroine I eventually snapped out of my pattern only to realize that the man I am engaging with is unable to change his ways (however I only do this once I have finally 'won them over'; and in a few instances once they became the male vampire). When this happened I received an abundance of self-esteem by leaving the relationship, feeling dignified and strong. That is until the next player lured me yet again. I remained pulled to this pattern until I got to a point where I detached from relationships altogether. This is when I became more of the butterfly and it was then that I discovered the dynamic of the hero/butterfly. For once I became dedicated to my independence and freedom I found myself being chased by numerous men who wanted to help me. I remember feeling during this time as though they were hypnotized by some image of me they held in their minds, that intimacy had never been achieved between us yet they were acting as if we were connected by deep experiences and years of interaction. Ultimately whatever part you are playing, be it the hero/heroine, player/butterfly, or the female/male vampire you are hypnotized because all people involved are unconscious of what they are really doing. And in fact the 'years of experience' projection is a tip off in some ways of where the feeling/emotion is truly coming from: their childhood experiences.

There is a paralysis that naturally comes with living out a pattern; it's like your conscious mind is halted in the moment so the pattern can unfold the way it is suppose to (just like with Alex, who literally couldn't 'see' or remember the warning signs). And what happens after a relationship pattern has ended and the person has grieved and grieved is that the intensity of the repressed emotion is lessened, but once that experience ends and time marches on the intensity will build again. Like a pot of water on a burner with a lid on: when it boils, it overflows but once it's brought back to normal temperature you wouldn't even know that there was any water at all in the closed pot. Re-entering a relationship pattern again is like putting the pot back on the burner, securing the lid and turning the dial to 'high'; it's only a matter of time until it violently overflows again. Then purpose of this book is about taking the figurative pot off of the burner and looking inside: this is the only way to transcend the pattern, the only way to create a new life with freedom and choice.

Before we begin to explore what our patterns are, and we begin the journey toward healing let's look at the patterns that aren't as stark as the one's outlined so far. Maybe you have read the universal roles and

don't quite feel as though any of them fit you, this is ok

because some patterns aren't as obvious as others. For

those of you that have ever been triggered by certain

types of people or feel as though in certain situations

you find yourself responding from repetitive, knee jerk

responses then the next chapters may help shed some

light on what is happening for you.

*P*atterns *vs. complexes*

If you don't really see any stark patterns in your

relationships, yet you know you aren't responding to

others from a place of freedom and choice then you

likely have core complexes that are keeping you

stuck. The difference between a pattern and a complex

is that a pattern is essentially a set script; where you

go out and find the same type of partner, where you

respond the same way and where the relationship ends

the same way. Whereas a complex indicates that there

are certain characteristics in others that really 'trigger'

you; these characteristics keep showing up in people you interact with and they limit you from responding freely in the moment. Patterns are mostly ignited from really painful and traumatic life events, whereas complexes exist in just about everyone who has ever been hurt or disappointed. Let's explore the differences between human patterns and complexes.

Carl Jung (1985) saw complexes as a core phenomenon in all human beings. Complexes are described by Jung as a 'node' in the unconscious; as he explains, "it can be imagined as a knot of unconscious feelings and beliefs, detectable indirectly, through behavior that is puzzling or hard to account for." The behavior that is puzzling can be seen in our relationships, and more specifically in how we relate to others. For example if someone was bullied for being short early in life, and this person was never able to fully process these emotions, this individual will likely develop a height complex when they are older. Their inability to process these emotions results in a 'node' or repressed energy because they aren't consciously aware of their repressed feelings around being bullied for how tall/short they are.

In mainstream society we use the term complex all the time, and it is important to understand that the concept essentially describes how repressed emotions live through interpersonal interactions. Further something that modern day society doesn't take into account is that the way complexes are born, like patterns, is from emotional repression and the activation of the reptilian brain.

Jung understood that repressed emotions remain alive within us and because they are alive they remain within us energetically. This energy remains blocked, it becomes a knot (Jung's 'node'), so like all energy that

is kept from moving, it will build as time goes by. And

as this energy builds it naturally increases its intensity

and its energy is magnified. Jung saw that the way

emotions remain blocked, the way they are held inside

without causing havoc, is through finding a way to be

released here and there unconsciously. And the way they

achieve this most effectively is through interpersonal

relationships. Clinical folks refer to this as becoming

'triggered' or projecting your 'stuff' onto the world.

The term 'trigger' is a perfect depiction of what is

really happening internally: when someone figuratively

hits on our energetic knot or node our autonomic

nervous system is set off and our reptilian brain steps in

to defend against what is happening. When we are

triggered by someone our repressed emotions come out

in the form of frustration or irritation at the other

person; we aren't really expressing the true 'reason' why we are having the emotional reaction. And since our reaction is not truly about the other person, but it's about our repressed emotions, we will continue to get triggered until we recognize where the trigger/complex comes from. Again the name of the game is to experience each moment completely, with as much awareness and choice as possible, when we are responding to another because a complex within us is triggered we are acting in an unconscious, reptilian brain way; hence we have little if any choice or awareness. Further, when the emotions are released unconsciously, the emotional energy is still within us because awareness is a vital step in processing the emotion completely.

Complexes take place when we have 'successfully' repressed certain emotions. What happens with complexes is that we become triggered by certain traits and personalities. These traits stir up what is repressed inside of us. Jung believed this phenomenon occurs so repressed emotions have a way to let off steam; in this way our emotional experience of being 'triggered' provides a medium in which we can release some of the built up energy. Jung believed that the way repressed emotions stay locked inside of us is if they are given times of catharsis; this process seems crucial because if there is not a channel then the emotions will threaten to break forth and come into the world. And since coming into the world is what the person is trying to not do (that's why the emotions are repressed to begin with) it makes sense that the human condition would develop a mechanism for keeping this from happening. After all we are repressing our emotions because we are unable to really express what we are feeling during a traumatic moment, and if our emotions don't really go away, then we are in a catch 22; we have to be able to do something with them.

Freud coined the term repression in order to explain how we hold emotions inside, and he was the first to highlight that when we repress we do it unconsciously (Freud, 1965). Freud's theory was born during the birth of the 1900's, in the midst of an era of reform and intellectual reasoning. In Freud's mind repression was absolutely necessary for successful adaptation to society, however what we are realizing now is that repression, while it may be adaptive when it occurs, is inevitably the impetus to symptoms in both the body and in human relationships. The 2nd law of thermodynamics dictates that energy stored, that is not 'used', will inevitably lead to entropy; where the system will begin to experience chaos, disorder and disorganization. Extrapolating this to the human experience, the more energy we have repressed the more disorder or dis-ease we will experience. In this day and age, with the evolution of consciousness, we are realizing that repression will lead to imbalance because we are blocking ourselves from expressing who we really are in the moment. Complexes are a symptom of this dis-order. This can be seen by the fact that when 'triggered' we are reacting to others as if they are someone else. Complexes trigger repressed emotions inside of us as well as activate reptilian responses, so instead of experiencing the relationship in the here and now we are really experiencing our past scars, where neither yourself or the other can be 'real' in the interaction.

As was discussed, Jung saw the way repression establishes its ability to function is through using interpersonal relationship 'moments' as a mode of

catharsis; and this happens through defense

mechanisms such as projection . The term 'projection'

refers to the phenomena when an individual projects

their own repressed emotional complexes onto another

person; like a video projector throwing images of a

movie on a wall. They then react to the traits in the

other person in highly emotional ways; in this they are

really reacting to the repressed material inside of them

as opposed to the other person in the here and now. It

would be like looking at images projected on a wall and

mistaking the wall for the images themselves. This

'mistake' in perception is the essence of projection.

Further the crux of this defense mechanism hinges on

the ability to project our repressed emotions outward so

we can achieve a mode of catharsis without ever really

processing the emotion(s); for we aren't achieving true

understanding and acceptance of the emotion. And if we project our emotions outwardly we never really 'own' our emotions and our repression remains in tact. This is what projection does: it places emotions *outside* of us and serves to keep us unaware that the emotions are really repressed *inside* of us. After all if we are focusing on the other person, then we really don't have the time to focus on ourselves. Let's look more closely at how emotional repression uses complexes in everyday life.

People develop core complexes around their emotions at a young age; looking at the previous example where the individual (who I will call Rob) felt inadequate because he was shorter than average. Rob was teased by both his siblings and peers because he wasn't as tall as his peers. What happened with Rob is that his feelings of shame and inadequacy became so repressed that he developed a complex around being short. Complexes come to be because a person keeps experiencing negative events associated with a certain trait (for this Rob the negative experience was being teased). Rob was unable to processes his emotions around these events so he repressed his feelings of shame and inadequacy. How this showed up later in life for Rob is that he began projecting these feelings onto other people. When he sees other people having issues with their height or even appearance he experiences an emotional charge. Rob has reported feeling annoyed and angry when he encounters these types of situations. What is happening here is that when he gets triggered he is solely focusing on the other person's experience; he becomes annoyed because they are mirroring his feelings of inadequacy and shame. Yet his anger and annoyance aren't really about the other person's feelings of inadequacy as much as it's about his own feelings of inadequacy. Now because he is placing or projecting his feelings of inadequacy onto the other person he doesn't have to confront his feelings of adequacy. Not only that but he achieves some release by projecting his feelings onto someone else and having an emotional reaction directed toward that other person. It's as if he is revealing what is really happening inside of him as well; if he gets angry at the other person, he is likely angry with himself for feeling a sense of shame. This is how complexes use relationships. And this is how relationships provide a mirror for what complexes we have operating inside of us, again giving us an opportunity to begin to heal these unprocessed emotions. We can also see that complexes, keep us somewhat stuck and blocked from being fully free in the moment. For we aren't responding to others as they are but we are responding to them, again, as we are.

Our complexes ultimately limit us from achieving healthy intimate relationships because what happens with complexes is that both people never really have the chance to connect authentically in the moment. Once we project our emotions onto another person we are no longer seeing the other person for who they really are. As Jung (1985) noted, "the effect of projection is to isolate the subject from his environment, since instead of a real relation to it there is only an illusionary one" (p. 92). Essentially when we are operating from a complex our unprocessed emotions get in the way from really interacting with an open mind. When we live out our complexes in our adult lives we remain blocked from really living freely with choice; and we remain blocked from ever

connecting intimately with another person. We end up

having illusionary relationships instead of truly

interacting from a place of authenticity. Let's look at

some more examples of what complexes look like in

real life.

Complexes in the flesh

There was a woman who came to disown her dependency needs because in her childhood climate it was adaptive for her to be independent and self-sufficient. In fact whenever she would behave in a needy manner her parents would criticize her behavior, telling her not to be so clingy. It's interesting how a certain trait becomes ingrained as being 'bad' or unacceptable if it violates a family rule. In this family there was an unspoken rule that nobody should be dependent, as independence was a valued trait. This little girl had numerous interactions that really drove home this point, so what she came to do was to repress her dependency needs and behavior in order to adapt to her family. Not only that but she also repressed her feelings of rejection and shame during interactions where she was criticized for being too needy or clingy. As she grew older she would often cry by herself in her room when she was sad, inherently because she knew that sadness made her seem needy. As an adult, she began to disconnect with feelings of sadness all together and she became highly independent; also she never cried in front of others, and rarely cried by herself (these behaviors became a solidified neural pathway: thus they were second nature and reflexive). Predictably what began to happen for her was that when she encountered people that displayed their feelings of sadness and dependency openly, she would experience a potent emotional reaction: they would irritate and frustrate her. At first she did not understand why these people would rub her this way; after all she would get triggered even when she first met someone. What we can see on the outside is that this woman is clearly operating out of a complex; she becomes annoyed with these individuals not because of who they are but because they hold characteristics that have been disowned and repressed within her. Now we have to appreciate that because of her complex, this woman won't be able to get to know these people and she won't be able to really share who she is either because the dynamic will be ruled by her complex. She will naturally see in them what she doesn't like in herself and her emotional reaction will get in the way of connecting intimately with them. Once we are responding from a complex, it's like we are unconsciously going through the motions; which again is because the encounter is triggering repressed emotions and thus we are unconsciously responding from a solidified neural pathway.

Another element of a complex that is really interesting is that the woman mentioned above will likely encounter this characteristic in individuals again and again in her life. What happens is that her psyche will attract these 'types' of people until her unconscious complex is resolved. This is her psyche's way of trying to release the emotionally repressed energy as well as trying to get her to eventually heal her wounds and complete the repressed emotional loops of expression associated with her wounds. Looking at the psyche as being driven to heal itself, it draws those individuals who will bring up repressed emotions that are incomplete and unhealed. Essentially we draw to us those people that represent the most opportune interactions for the most amount of healing.

Now you may ask how you can tell if you are operating from one of your complexes. The answer is that you can tell if a complex is operating because of the strong affect that gets triggered within you. Like the woman in the above example that would feel strong emotions of annoyance and frustration when she was confronted with dependent behavior. The emotional reaction she was having to dependent characteristics was so strong and out of proportion to the situation that we know a complex has been triggered. Also you will feel like the response or feeling you have is outside of your control; this of course is because when you are triggered you are coming from a reptilian brain, knee jerk, response- which is necessarily outside of your control- it just happens. You quite simply aren't in your neocortex, you don't have access to higher brain functions, where choice lies. Have you ever had a time when an acquaintance you were interacting with, maybe even someone you just met, gets on your nerves in an unspeakable way? It is likely that they triggered a complex within you, after all if it is a random stranger and you get triggered you should be suspicious (strong emotional affect shouldn't be triggered by strangers). This is when someone just walks into the room and says something completely innocuous and for whatever reason you want to lash out or leave the room altogether. Further, when a complex is triggered we are also unable to step outside the situation in order to take an objective stance; complexes make it so we get completely pulled into a dynamic that is conflicting and we respond to the conflict unconsciously. Let's look at another example of a complex that really highlights this point.

Let's look at how a complex would operate with a man who is very extraverted and social and who was raised in a context where it was good to be outgoing and the life of the party. As a child this individual was criticized when he was somber and withdrawn, and this occurred pretty much until this man was in his teens. Soon after he began to figure out (on an unconscious level) that being withdrawn and mellow inherently violates a family rule. So what ended up happening is that he repressed his feelings during these childhood experiences and more mellow and introverted ways of being come to represent a complex later in his life. As an adult, this man naturally draws to himself individuals that enjoy solitude and tend to be withdrawn. In fact he even tends to attract romantic partners with these characteristics. And sure enough when the other person begins to get mellow and express a desire for solitude he starts to feel extremely angry and frustrated. In fact even when he meets an individual that is introverted he finds himself wanting to roll his eyes or shake the person. Here we are teed off that there is a complex present because of the strong affect he experiences toward relative strangers. We also know it's a complex when he reveals that he tends to draw these types of people into his life. When asked what is happening for him when he interacts with these individuals, he tells me that he feels as though its wrong for the other person to have alone time or to become internally focused. This feeling is key because we can really see how his reaction to the other person is mirroring what he was told as a child. What happens then is that when he interacts with an introvert he will naturally start to feel as though a rule is being violated. These types of relationships serve to keep his complex in place because he achieves catharsis through channeling his repressed emotions within his reaction to the other, while remaining unconscious of the complex itself. Further he also gets to act out the process of fighting this undesired or taboo trait externally. This struggle is already operating inside of him, but now it's externalized in his relationships. Ultimately, the externalization of this conflict is actually the perfect opportunity for him to see what his repressed emotions are as well as the perfect opportunity to begin to heal/process the emotions that created the complex to begin with.

For the extrovert, the pattern of attracting introverted people will continue to repeat itself until he becomes aware of his repressed emotions. And it will continue to repeat itself until he also heals the emotions

associated with his childhood experiences and then

chooses to respond differently in the present. In order

to do this he first must express the shame around

feeling rejected and experience/understand/accept the

repressed emotions from his childhood (thereby

allowing the repressed emotions to complete their loop

of expression). Then he can do something different:

he can start to give himself permission to have some

down time or to turn down social invitations when he

really wants to be home. This will enable him to really

learn new and authentic ways of being and his complex

will then be resolved. What he will find after he does

this intrapersonal work is that he won't really be

'triggered' by the introvert anymore, the energy and

annoyance will just go away. What's even more

interesting is that once you heal a complex it's almost

like you never had it to begin with, it vanishes and you suddenly 'forget' about the complex all together because the emotions associated with it are no longer present (the energy vanishes when processed).

These have been examples of how complexes come to life in interpersonal relationships. The above two examples are similar to one another because they both involved disowned character traits; the woman was not owning her dependency needs and the man was disowning his introverted ways of being. This is a common phenomena for most people, as we all have been taught to be a certain way over another, however complexes can also show up in the reverse process, where the individual is triggered by individuals who actually mirror the traits they call their own. Let's look at an example of how this may show up out in the world.

Complexes II

Have you ever notice that people who are similar in personality actually repel one another? Ever see a father and son who vow to never speak to one another, who tell others over and over again how difficult the other one is, only to reflect on their relationship and muse over how similar they are? I have a friend, Rick, who is extremely opinionated and passionate about his political views. Actually he is opinionated and passionate about anything he believes in. He is the type of man that would not hesitate for a moment to start up a heated dialogue in a restaurant, school or church. He knows what he believes and he expresses it. Now, his son, Collin, is also this way; he is just as verbal and passionate about his beliefs. Unfortunately the two drive each other crazy because they don't see eye to eye on numerous topics of importance to both of them. You can often hear Rick talking about Collin, his son, and declaring him to be stubborn and pig- headed. Likewise if you talk to Collin you would hear the same thing; this time about his dad. Each of them feels the other is so opinionated and closed-minded, and each is driven absolutely crazy by this proclaimed fault on the others' part. Interestingly, when you step outside of the situation you can clearly see that what drives my friend crazy about his son: is really what drives himself crazy about himself. Likewise, what Collin loathes about his father is really Collin's reaction to his own behavior. What they see in the other, what drives them crazy, is really what they see in themselves. And while it is good to have beliefs and feel strongly and passionately about them I think we would all agree that being close minded is definitely not a healthy stance.

Fundamentally when we are closed down to new ideas we aren't really being present and in the moment (therefore not authentically experiencing what is really happening: which is again the name of the game). Rick and Collin are inherently keyed in to this truism as they get extremely outraged by each other's behaviors, but if they just reflected on their own complex around needing to be right they could diffuse a lot of emotional intensity between them. You see like all other complexes, Rick was raised in an environment where it was highly valued for him to be verbal and expressive about his beliefs and he was rewarded for being intelligent and knowledgeable on most topics. These experiences (albeit seemingly positive) drove him to ALWAYS be right on anything that was being discussed, to a point where he doesn't even listen to anyone else. We can see how these childhood experiences set him up for developing a core complex around being right. This complex operates in interest of continuously giving Rick self-esteem and a sense of personal value. This drive is not only a natural defense against ever being wrong and violating a family taboo, but also against breaking a fundamental aspect of his self-identity.

Because Collin was raised by Rick, he followed by example and learned the same unspoken rule and the same way of being. So naturally they will come to trigger one another as the other has become a perfect mirror for what is being repressed inside of them. After all, we all need to feel like we can be human, that we can be wrong and still be lovable. Due to their childhood this sense of acceptance is not really felt by either men; and as Rick looked toward his father for approval, so too does Collin look to Rick. So until Rick begins to heal this complex it will be next to impossible for him to give his son the unconditional acceptance Collin longs for. Of course Collin could heal this wound on his own too; in the end, it is the work we do on ourselves that facilitates our own healing. It's not about getting our father or mother or sister or brother to change it is really about discovering what is keeping us from changing that offers us the greatest opportunity to make our own lives drastically more fulfilling. So for both my friend and his son the first step to healing their complexes really involves self- aware: understanding that they have a complex operating to begin with, followed by healing the wounds that created the complex and coming to a place where they can live their lives with more balance and ultimately more choice.

For all the examples shared above the more the individuals process their unhealed wounds from childhood, the more freedom they have to live their life in the here and now. Just as we already touched on in reviewing the nature of emotions, the individual needs to discover the origin of their repressed emotions, feel the emotions, understand, accept and then move on. And you will know when you have successfully achieved this, because the traits and personalities that use to trigger you, all the sudden have no impact on your emotions what so ever. In fact you may get to a place where you feel genuine compassion and understanding for those who possess your disowned, or overly owned, traits. And you may also notice, that you are no longer attracting these types of individuals into your life anymore; that emotional magnet all the sudden losses its livelihood and vigor.

These were examples of what complexes look like in interpersonal relationships. I wanted to touch on this phenomenon because of the impact complexes have on any relationship in your life. Complexes provide a medium for discovering what family rules and/or traumas have impacted who you have become, as well as discovering the neural pathways that have limited you from truly interacting with others from a place of choice. They differ from patterns in that they really correspond to specific character traits; whereas a pattern is a whole slew of behaviors. Further within patterns lie a lot of complexes that show up in relationships in predictable ways; thus it was important to review the nature of complexes themselves. Now the next and most fundamental step to this entire process of self-exploration: how we go about undoing our patterns, completing our emotional loops and healing our past traumas.

*H*ealing patterns & complexes

We can do it differently, as locked as we may seem in repeating our past mistakes. As long as we are able to look at our life history and to examine the patterns that pull us, we have the ability to wake up from our reflexive, reptilian responses in relationships and to begin to create a new day filled with the potential for love and growth. Let's look at the path that can lead us to greater freedom; that can aid us in healing from our pasts so we don't have to make the same unconscious decisions and we don't

have to feel the same pain in relationships ever again.

The way to begin healing a pattern or complex

is through first discovering what the pattern or complex

is and then figuring out where it came from. Once you

have identified what your complexes or patterns are (be

it a hero/heroine, player/butterfly, or female/male

vampire- or possibly a combo) you then need to

identify the first initial scar that created the pattern or

complex. Once you begin the journey of self-reflection

around your childhood experiences you will naturally

begin to delve into the repressed emotions around those

specific moments in time. It seems even beginning to

reflect upon these moments you will inevitably begin to

get in touch with the emotional responses you

repressed; in fact you will likely re-experience these

emotions in one form or another. And what's pretty

amazing is that the universe will provide opportunities for this.

Numerous friends, colleagues, clients, as well as myself, have discovered that as soon as we start exploring past traumas, we literally run into people associated with the trauma within days of our exploration. This happened to me personally each time I delved into another traumatic moment. Expect that this may happen to you as well. You may also 'coincidently' rent a movie or hear a song on the radio that brings up the feelings you repressed in response to the specific trauma. Maybe somebody will call you or you will hear a name that is associated with your past memory. I look at all this as the psyche's way of trying to heal itself. Now exactly how this happens; whether it's the universe literally working with your unconscious or it's your unconscious paying attention to specific stimuli in order to bring it to your awareness, is a whole book in itself. But I will say that if you do experience this, just know that you are not alone and it's a common occurrence for most people who are working on healing repressed memories. I actually look at it as a really good sign that you are on the right track!

It is important to note that maybe you don't have an extreme pattern, maybe you aren't a hero or a player, maybe you fall somewhere in between. Perhaps you have childhood wounds but they aren't as stark as the stories told in this book, this is o.k. because even subtle patterns and complexes can be uncovered through certain exercises and self-reflection. Let's begin to look at where you are at this point in your life and let's first do this by looking at your current relationships and unconscious triggers.

*E*xercise #1: your 'triggers' & complexes

Let's first start to explore similarities in characteristics between your current romantic partner and childhood relationships, in order to get an idea of what your 'triggers' and complexes are:

1) First I want you to get out a pen and write down all the different characteristics of your partner that seem to trigger or create a strong emotional reaction in you. Once you have done this I want you to begin to reflect on each characteristic and ask yourself who else in your life has these

characteristics? Maybe your mom holds a few, perhaps your dad holds most, maybe even your siblings or a close aunt. Now once you have pinpointed who in your distant past resonates with your present partner I want you to write the specific name by your partner along with the characteristic. (E.g. if your partner is controlling and so is/was your dad write dad next to controlling and your partner's name).

2) Once you have completed #1, I want you to write down the names of other partners you have had in your life especially ones that broke your heart (or visa versa) or triggered you. Now next to these names write another list of characteristics that really ignited an emotional fire you in. Once you have done this again

think back to your youth and write down who

else had each of these characteristics (repeating

step #1). Now once you have completed this

you are ready for the harder part (harder

because it really involves a lot of emotional

honesty-as well as looking at some difficult and

maybe painful memories).

3) The next step is to go to each characteristic and

names from your childhood that you listed in #1

and #2 and remember back to the first

experience you had that involved this

characteristic. For example if you get really

triggered by 'neediness' and you wrote the

name of your sister down, think back to when

you first experienced her neediness. Remember

when they really displayed whatever the

characteristic is that now triggers you. If you

wrote your own name down remember the first time you displayed this characteristic. Once you are aware of the situation (and it may take a few days or even weeks for a clear memory to manifest) I want you to take a third person perspective and really see yourself in the situation. From here I want you to ask yourself "how did I respond to this person when they were displaying this characteristic"?. And "how did the world respond to me when I was displaying this behavior". For example if the characteristic is anger maybe you responded by withdrawing and becoming aloof. Maybe you responded to neediness by becoming frustrated and angry. Maybe others responded to your sadness by criticizing you or withdrawing. Whatever your response was, or other people's responses where, I want you to observe what your response did to your body. Did it make you tense up or turn your head down? Did you respond physically by clenching your fists or tightening your chest and jaw? What did you do during this event? Write this information down for each characteristic and childhood experience. This exercise helps you to tap into the emotions in your body, and by just remembering how it felt you will naturally begin to bring them to the surface.

4) Next I want you to remember what you told yourself during these past situations if you can. Did you tell yourself that you deserve what is happening, that you are bad or worthless or maybe you told yourself you will never share your heart again? Or maybe you just withdrew

and disconnected entirely from the experience so you don't remember telling yourself anything. Whatever you recall is o.k.; this is just a preliminary exploration. The more you reflect the more material will surface.

5) This next piece is crucial for understanding what you really needed during your past traumas. I want you to lie back and again imagine the event from your childhood that has surfaced. From here I want you to imagine receiving what you needed from your environment. Maybe you can have the person involved in 'hurting you' reach out and provide comfort. Or perhaps you need to imagine the 'grown up' you coming to your rescue. Envision the memory in a way that feels 'right' and fulfilling. After you complete this visually

I would recommend journaling your new story and then perhaps expressing the new images in the form of art. By doing this you are literally creating new neural pathways; your mind literally cannot distinguish between imaginary and real life experiences.

It is not unusual to experience some intense emotions during these exercises, in fact if you do it's actually a good sign that you are ready to really process and release them. It may be good to seek out a therapist or coach that can help you to process the repressed material as well; this also provides a great forum for being able to reflect on them, thereby allowing you to complete the emotional loop and let the emotion go. Journaling, art work or body work (such as massage or chiropractic) can also aid in releasing the emotions that will likely manifest.

6) The next thing I want you to reflect on is how you are now in your more current life with individuals who display the characteristics you have written down. Are you still responding in the same way? Maybe you developed another coping skill that took over the initial one you developed in your youth. Write this down as well. By now you are likely seeing the parallels from your past with your current circumstances which means you are getting a sense of what your complexes and repressed emotions are. Again I would definitely recommend discussing this with a therapist, close friend or family member or journaling, just to achieve some insight into what you have uncovered.

I know a woman who would first cry in response to feeling neglected in her childhood only to eventually detach herself from her relationships once she got older; she developed a coping skill that actually joined with the characteristics that initially hurt her as a child: where she becomes emotionally detached when she really wants to cry. This is a very common phenomenon, there are so many different ways we adapt to our life situation but the one thing that is universal is that our original response, if it is causing us to repeat the same relationships, indicates an unhealed wound inside of us. These unhealed responses are what get us to form our patterns later in life. This brings us to our next step. This is when we shall explore what your specific pattern is in your adult relationships.

*E*xercise #2: *your childhood*

nest

---

1) I want you to again think about the last two or
   preferably three significant relationships you
   have had. Again get out a pen and piece of
   paper and write down the names of the
   individual whom who had these relationships
   with. Now write one word that describes each
   relationship; act like it was a movie and ask
   yourself what would the title be? What was the
   overall theme of the relationship?

2) Now I want you to write down the emotions you

associate with this relationship, if they varied

according the stages of the relationship (i.e., the

beginning, middle and end) then write down the

order of their occurrence. Do this for each

relationship. (Note: if anger comes up I want you

to think about what emotion is underneath the

anger, for example if you were angry that your

boyfriend cheated on you maybe you really felt

betrayed or hurt or sad deep down).

3) Now I want you to start to reflect on each

emotion you wrote down and next to each

emotion I want you to think about the first time

you experienced the given emotion with great

intensity. Think about the first really significant

experience you had with the given feeling in

your childhood and write that down next to the

emotion.

4) If you are having a difficult time recalling the emotions in #3 I want you to write a story about your parents/caregivers' relationship, what was the theme of their story, how did you respond to what was happening with them?

By now you should start to see a pattern emerging. Maybe you notice a theme of rejection and loss; and you have noted that you first felt these feelings when a parent left or died or got sick. Just notice what comes up for you as you discover this information as well. We will go into ways you can begin to process these emotions and the key piece right now is learning what your pattern is and discovering where it really comes from.

*E*xercise #3: your relationship patterns

1) Maybe you have already identified with one of the patterns mentioned; maybe you know you are a hero or a butterfly. If you know your pattern I want you to write it down in big letters. If you don't identify with any of the patterns mentioned try to capture your way of being in relationships in a few words (what is the overarching attitude; are you super easygoing and nonchalant/ do you try to make everyone

around you laugh thereby playing the jokester role?).

2) Next I want you to write a story about where this pattern comes from in the third person; at what moment in time was this pattern first born? For example if you are a heroine I want you to tell the story of where your drive to save or win your partner was first ignited, remember what happened way back when. If you are a player, ask yourself when did you decide to not take any relationship seriously? Also remember to look back even 10 years ago and see if you had another pattern that you took on back then and if so ask yourself the same questions? Just begin writing a story around the given event and think

of ways your pattern may have been ignited
during that time.

3) After you have written your story I want you to
look back and try to remember what you told
yourself when the story was unfolding (the story
of your childhood nest), what did you resolve to
do to prevent the story from repeating itself in
your life? Some of you may not be able to
recall, that's o.k. for now because it might come
to you later (if you were too young to recall- just
write down what you think you would have told
yourself).

4) Look at what you told yourself (from question
#3) and see how it applies to your current
relationships, how does it show up in your
relationships now? Write this down next to the

list of names you wrote down, and write down how it showed up with each person; maybe you told yourself you would never trust anyone again, and in your last relationship this really showed up through suspiciousness (write down suspiciousness next to the name of your last relationship). Start seeing the parallels between your childhood experiences and your adult relationships.

5) Now I want you to see yourself as you were when your first painful experience occurred and imagine that the younger you is the one involved in your more current relationships. What is the overarching emotion this child has during these last few relationships? Viewing yourself as a child interacting now, frees you to

see your underlying issues with greater clarity;

and it gets you closer to really seeing the

parallel between your adult encounters and your

childhood nest. Do you have a theme of loss

and sadness? Where do these emotions come

from? What event in your past are they really

tied too? Once you have been able to see what

repressed emotions may have influenced your

current relationships you can begin to

understand why you have made the choices you

have in your romantic partners.

*E*xercise #4: *healing your patterns & complexes*

Once you uncover what your pattern is and where it comes from you will begin to understand what has motivated your adult relationships. Now you need to ask yourself: what needs to be healed and processed? What event(s) from your past has emotions that have not been processed? Once you do this and you discover what past event or relationship was the impetus to your pattern you can then engage in a few different exercises to begin the processing of any repressed emotions. Review each step and I would recommend spacing out the exercises over a period of time (which will give you more time to process the emotions themselves).

1. Write a letter to the individual with whom you had the difficult experience with (you don't have to send the letter-I actually recommend you don't- it is merely a way to get to the emotions beneath this relationship)

2. Once you have written a letter to the given person (without sending it) - I want you to write a letter back to yourself, as if you were this person, and give yourself validation for your feelings; tell yourself what you would have wanted the other person might tell you.

3. Now lie back and close your eyes and imagine yourself as a child during the given trauma. Really feel the emotions you

experienced and become aware of the thoughts you may have had. Once you are really 'in' the experience I want you to imagine a stronger, loving and comforting person coming to the 'childhood you'. Maybe this person was a coach you had as a child or an aunt, this person could even be the adult you. Imagine giving to this child exactly what you needed during this time. Stay with this visualization for as long as you need to. You may want to give yourself a week even to really let this step absorb into your experience.

4. Next I want you to go back yet again to your memories and ask yourself how you would have responded to the situation if you felt

safe and supported. Ask yourself how you have responded if you weren't coming from fear? It may even be helpful to think of someone in your life that you admire, who you consider loving and strong, and ask yourself how they would have responded in this situation? (Sometimes it is helpful to interject someone else into our memory in order to achieve some emotional distance and gain clarity).

5.   Now I want you to take a look at the story you wrote about your pattern and how it developed in your past, and I want you to rewrite the story; with the event still happening but this time have yourself respond in the way you described in #4.

6. Now look at this event from a higher perspective, from you higher self, from your spiritual self or God (whatever you conceive Him/It to be) and tell yourself from this perspective what the purpose of this life experience was. What can you gain from this event? How will this event make you stronger, wiser etc..? Now write down, in the words of this higher perspective, what It/He/She would tell you?

Working through unconscious complexes and patterns is not just a theoretical exercise it is something that necessarily needs to be done interactively but you can begin to invite healing to happen through increasing your awareness of your childhood wounds and present triggers. These exercises provide the space for you to begin to go inside and explore your past traumas, in order to really understand where you have been, where you are and what you want to do differently. Remember it's not about placing blame, it's about becoming aware. Nobody is to blame because nothing is really wrong it's all a part of our journey toward wholeness and freedom.

Application of our awareness is a vital step toward healing from our past, it is a necessary step toward creating a new life here and now, where you step out of the past once and for all and come into the present moment. Let's look at the next steps you can take to bring yourself to the next level, the place where you can start creating and attracting relationships from a place of choice.

Transcending your patterns & complexes

Once you get to a place where you know what your patterns are, and you feel like you are ready to move beyond where you have been, and you feel as though you have processed many of your incomplete emotional loops you can literally start to create new neural pathways that will enable you to have different experiences in your relationships. This piece is actually key in undoing your previous patterns, because what has been found in neurological studies is that the way we change old behavior is not by undoing the solidified neural pathways; rather the way we change behavior is by creating new pathways in the mind and through repetition we can have the new pathways replace the old. Through certain exercises that enable us to focus on what we want (instead of what we don't) we are able to make it so these pathways dominate- thereby de-strengthening the old habitual ways of behaving. It reminds me of a story one of my colleges shared about why it's so important to focus on what we want in life; over focusing on what we don't. She shared that this hit her literally one time when she was riding her bike down a street lined with these really low sitting branches. As she was coming down the path she noticed this huge branch hanging down in front of her. In her mind she figured out that she could easily duck beneath the branch and make it through fine, but what did she do instead? She focused on the branch itself: the exact area she wanted to avoid and sure enough she ran right into the branch and ended up crashing. The next time she rode down the street what she did instead was to focus on the way through the branches and sure enough when she did this she made it through no problem. Likewise, once we get to a place where we healed our old patterns, what we really need to do is to focus on what we want in our lives and how we want to behave. Instead of looking back or perceiving new interactions with our old lens, we need to look through the branches and see where the new opportunities to interact differently lie. Not only that but neuropsychologists have discovered that the way to dismantle our reptilian brain responses, and to deactivate our autonomic nervous system is by harnessing our sense of vision and hope. MRI studies have literally shown that when individuals are in a flight/fight response pattern they are no longer utilizing the neocortex. This is the area of the brain that enables us to come up with solutions, to be proactive and to make decisions based on consequences and logic. But what they also discovered was that as soon as these individuals were guided to start thinking about their dreams, about their vision and about what is possible in their life their neocortex lit up like a Christmas tree. This piece is key in understanding how to create new ways of responding, and the way to do it is to start visualizing how you want your life to be. There are some exercises that can guide you in beginning the process toward creating new neural pathways and behaviors and we will go into that right now.

*E*xercise #5: *creating your future*

---

1) Think about your most ideal relationship. What are the qualities of this relationship? I want you to sit back and meditate on this question. It may take you a few minutes, hours, days or even weeks to answer it, but really think about what the perfect relationship looks like to you. Allow yourself to believe it can happen too, don't let doubt come in at all, I want you to fully dream the most amazing relationship possibly.

2) Next I want you to journal about what you discovered in #1; describe in detail what the

relationship looks like. How do the two of you interact, how do you *feel* in the relationship? What qualities does your partner have, what do the two of you do together. Paint the most vivid picture of this. Really focus on the feeling more than logical details- you want to transport yourself there- creating new neural pathways in the moment (again the brain can't distinguish between imagery and real life experiences)

3) After you have completed #2 along with journaling your ideal relationship I want you to try to set aside time each day, even if only for a few minutes and go back to these images, play it in your head over and over again. If you are an artist and want to paint, draw or color something to represent this do that. Also vision boards that

depict what you want your life to look like are

an awesome way to really bring the image to

life (use magazines to cut out images that

embody what your ideal life would look like).

The key to this exercise is repetition- do #4, #5.

#6 etc…over and over again!

By visualizing your ideal life daily you are literally

creating new neural pathways, and remember the way

to undo old patterns/pathways in the mind is by creating

new dominate pathways. And the way to make a

pathway dominate is to use it as much as possible.

What is amazing about this is that even visualizing our

ideal interactions actually has the power to create new

neural pathways that will enable us to do it with others

in real life; what a better way to begin a new behavior

then to start to practice it in our mind. I would suggest

imagining your perfect relationship before you go to

bed at night or when you are stressed out, do it when you have a free moment and do it as much as possible. You will know you are on the right track by the way you feel; if you get excited and feel inspired and alive you are doing it 'right'.

Now if you start to feel yourself slip back into your old way of relating, this is ok and it's almost to be expected. You can't change something deeply ingrained over night, but if you are healing your past scars, releasing repressed emotions, completing their loop of expression and doing visualization techniques in order to create new neural pathways eventually what you want will come to fruition. Another thing to remember is that your childhood nest is what's familiar, a relationship that is healthy, intimate and mature may feel a little odd at first, it's like you have to retrain yourself. But when you feel like you are getting off track, sit down again and envision your perfect relationship all over again. I know people that have had to do this a zillion of times, and you know what, it doesn't end. Life is dynamic and ever changing, so if we want to keep having healthy authentic relationships we have to keep doing what it takes to bring that to us. And we have to keep doing what it takes to keep us in a space of openness and vulnerability (two qualities that are key for maintaining intimate relationships). Think of it like muscles, in order to maintain them you have to keep doing activities that stimulate and feed them. It's the same thing with neural pathways in the mind and new behaviors, although eventually it will start to feel way more second nature and reflexive.

*C*onclusion

I had a conversation the other day with my friend Joe and he hit the nail on the head when he mused that our childhood is all about preparing ourselves for adulthood, and adulthood is all about reliving and/or recovering from our childhood. The reality is that human development isn't as clear cut as some want to assume, we don't grow up into emotionally whole and healthy individuals at age 18 and successfully enter adulthood ready for intimacy and connection. The fact is that we are all human. And the nature of being human is to respond to situations the best way we know how. Our parents and our parents' parents responded to us with the tools they had in the moment. Hence there is rarely a person you will meet who does not carry with them scars from the past. In fact in many ways I believe that creating our childhood nests out in the world is really an opportunity to grow psychologically and spiritually.

When we begin to go within and we begin to explore our emotional past, we get the opportunity to tap into our true nature. Beyond what has happened to us, beyond our solidified neural pathways, lies a spiritual essence that is embedded within all of us. Within the darkness we find our light. So when we go within we are headed in the right direction. Perhaps the entire phenomenon of the human nest is really our spiritual calling to come back to ourselves. The more we look within the more we find exactly who we are.

So during moments of pain, of reliving past traumas, know that you are clearing away everything that limits you from truly being who you are meant to be. It's like the birthing of the butterfly. When we go inside we create a cocoon in which we can grieve, process and mourn. Once we release our repressed emotions we are suddenly free to break out of our old shell, our limiting neural pathways and patterns, and then we can begin to explore how we want to be in the world. From this we can begin to manifest relationships that enhance us and facilitate our journey toward wholeness and authenticity.

When we begin to consciously create our relationships we suddenly realize that we can bring to us precisely what we want. If you want to change what's happening on the outside, you must first change what is happening within. We have the power to manifest our wildest dreams all we need is the courage to begin our inward journey and to ultimately believe that we can have the relationships we really want. As Wayne Dyer put it, 'you will see it when you believe it'. As soon as you heal the traumas from yesterday you can truly live in the NOW. My hope is that after reading this each and every one of you will discover you do in fact have wings; and that the saying 'the sky is the limit' is actually one of the most accurate and profound statements ever made. Ultimately when we begin to tap into who we really are in the moment, connecting with others in a real and authentic way, we begin to truly learn how to fly.

R*eferences*

Freud, S. (1961/1989). *The future of illusion.* New York: W.W. Norton & Co.

Freud, S. (1950). *Totem and taboo.* New York: W.W. Norton & Co.

Freud, S. (1965). *The interpretation of dreams.* New York: Avon Books.

Hendrix, H. (1988). *Getting the love you want: A guide for couples.* New York: Harper Perennial Publishers.

Jung, C. G. (1985). *The Essential Jung*. New York: Vantage Books

Kurtz, R. (1990). *Body-centered psychotherapy: The Hakomi method*. Mendocino: LifeRhythm.

Macnaughton, I. Ed. (1998) *Embodying the mind & minding the body: A collection of articles on family systems, bodydynamics, somatic developmental psychology, shock trauma, and spirituality.* Albany: Kreatic Press